WORLD WAR I for Kids

A History with 21 Activities

R. KENT RASMUSSEN

CHICAGO REVIEW PRESS

First edition
Published by Chicago Review Press, Incorporated
814 North Franklin Street
Chicago, Illinois 60610
ISBN 978-1-61374-556-4

Library of Congress Cataloging-in-Publication Data
Rasmussen, R. Kent.
    World War I for kids : a history with 21 activities / R. Kent Rasmussen. — First edition.
        pages cm
    Includes bibliographical references and index.
    Audience: Ages 9 and up.
    ISBN 978-1-61374-556-4 (trade paper)
    1. World War, 1914-1918—Juvenile literature. 2. World War, 1914-1918—Study and
teaching—Activity programs. 3. Creative activities and seat work—Juvenile literature.
    I. Title.

    D522.7R37 2014
    940.4—dc23

                                                                          2013037624

Cover and interior design: Monica Baziuk
Cover images: Library of Congress: Uncle Sam, mounted solier, Wilhelm II,
Women! propaganda poster, and *Luisitania* poster. National Archives and Records:
Children refugess and men leaving Camp Dix. *National Geographic* magazine (1917,
v. 31, p. 379): Men in trenches. iStockphoto: Biplane © breckeni; German helmet
© jsolie. Shutterstock: poppy flower © Chris Howey Author's collection: "Over There"
sheet music.
Interior illustrations: Jim Spence

Printed in the United States of America
5 4 3 2 1

To Bailey, Jackson, Zane, Miranda, Cosette,
Damon, Griffin, and Maggie:
may you and your generation never see another war.

CONTENTS

TIME LINE

1914 ☆

June 28   Austrian archduke Franz Ferdinand is assassinated in Serbia

July 6   Germany agrees to support Austria-Hungary against Serbia

July 28   Austria-Hungary declares war on Serbia; Russia begins to mobilize for war

August 1–4   Germany declares war on Russia, France, and Belgium

August 2–4   Germany invades Poland, Luxembourg, France, and Belgium; Great Britain declares war on Germany

August 7   British troops begin landing in France; French troops invade Alsace

August 10–13   France and Britain declare war on Austria-Hungary

August 19   United States formally declares its neutrality

August 21   Battle of the Ardennes

August 23   Japan declares war on Germany

August 26–29   Germans stop Russian advance into East Prussia at Battle of Tannenberg

August 28   British Royal Navy attacks German positions in Battle of Heligoland, also known as the Battle of the Bight

September 5   Britain, France, and Russia sign agreement not to seek separate peace

September 6–11   Allies stop German advance on Paris in First Battle of the Marne; trench warfare will soon begin

November 1   German naval squadron defeats British squadron off Chilean coast in the Battle of Coronel

November 5–6   Britain and France declare war on Turkey

November 11   German drive to the North Sea halted in First Battle of Ypres

December 8   German squadron defeated at Falkland Islands

December 25   British and German troops fraternize during a Christmas truce near Ypres in Belgium

1915 ☆

February 1   Germany announces beginning of submarine warfare

April–May   International Congress of Women at the Hague, Netherlands, seeks ways to end the war

April 25–January 26, 1916   Allied campaign at Gallipoli

April 22   Germans introduce chlorine gas at Second Battle of Ypres

May 7   British passenger liner *Lusitania* is sunk by German submarine

May 23–24   Italy declares war on Austria-Hungary

August 21   Italy declares war on Turkey

September 4–5   Tsar Nicholas II assumes command of all Russian forces

September 18   Germany stops submarine warfare

1916 ☆

February 21–December 18	Battle of Verdun
March 2	Germany resumes submarine warfare
April 23	Easter Rebellion in Ireland
May 17	British Parliament enacts military conscription
May 31	Naval Battle of Jutland
July–November	First Battle of the Somme
August 26	Italy declares war on Germany
August 31	Germany again stops submarine warfare
September 6	Central Powers form unitary supreme command
September 15	Britain introduces tanks at the Somme
October 15	Germany resumes submarine warfare
November 7	Wilson is re-elected US president on an antiwar platform
November 21	Emperor Francis Joseph dies

1917 ☆

January 9	Germany again resumes unrestricted submarine warfare
March 11–15	Russian Revolution begins after Tsar Nicholas abdicates
April 6	United States declares war on Germany; other Western Hemisphere nations follow
May 15	Pétain assumes overall command of French army
May 26	First US troops arrive in France
June 6	Sailors in German navy begin to revolt

July–November	Battle of Passchendale
November 8	Lenin and Trotsky form Bolshevik government in Russia
December	British troops occupy Jerusalem
December 22–March 3, 1918	Russia negotiates peace settlement with Central Powers

1918 ☆

January 8	Wilson presents "Fourteen Points" to US Congress
July 8	Tsar Nicholas II and his family are murdered
November 7–8	German revolution begins in Munich
November 9	German emperor Wilhelm II abdicates
November 11	Armistice ends fighting in Europe
November 14	German forces in East Africa surrender, ending combat

1919 ☆

June 28	Treaty of Versailles is signed

1920 ☆

November 15	League of Nations opens first session of General Assembly

INTRODUCTION

WORLD WAR I may have been the most important turning point of the 20th century. It was not as large and devastating a conflict as World War II would be, but it did even more to shape the world as it is today. It ravaged most of Europe and destroyed four empires while also creating many new nations. It triggered the Russian Revolution and laid the bases for Balkan and Middle Eastern conflicts that remain unresolved today. Most significantly, perhaps, it gave Germany grievances that Adolf Hitler's Nazi movement would exploit in its rise to power and thereby contribute to the Holocaust and World War II. Indeed, the roots of that later world war are so deeply embedded in the first that the second world war might justly be considered a continuation of World War I.

World War I also raised the United States to the status of a world power and inspired the creation of the League of Nations, the predecessor of the United Nations. In addition, it fundamentally transformed military combat by introducing weapons of unprecedented destructive power and by taking combat closer to civilian populations than ever before. It revolutionized naval warfare and gave the world aerial warfare. Meanwhile, the war's impact on the home fronts of the nations involved set in motion vast social changes, extending democracy, giving more women the vote, and helping to liberate women in the workplace.

The war began in 1914 with plans based on 19th-century military thinking. By the time it ended four years later, it had become a high-tech 20th-century war whose advances would influence the way future wars would be fought. The most obvious military changes it introduced were in weaponry. These included more lethal machine guns, longer-range and more accurate artillery, more powerful battleships, deadly poison gases, mechanized tanks, submarines capable of sinking ships, and armed aircraft. Each of these innovations forced changes in tactics and strategy and inspired further advances.

Change in History

CHANGE IS the essence of history, and World War I offers a rich workshop for exploring historical change. This book's central goals are to explain how the war arose, how it differed from earlier wars, and how changes brought by large-scale warfare can have far-reaching effects. World War I is important not merely because of the scale of its fighting or the destruction it brought but also because of the sweeping changes it forced on the world. War is always about much more than the purely military matters of weaponry and fighting. World War I destroyed, transformed, and even created entire nations, altering their political systems, economies, and cultures.

In studying wars in history, what really matters is not so much which nations won or lost but what kind of changes the wars brought. It is sometimes not completely clear who won a war. The question of who won World War I may seem easy to answer because the governments of Germany and other Central Powers either surrendered or collapsed. The reality, however, is more complicated. Germany's government did formally surrender. However, many Germans thought their military had actually won the war. They believed the military had been betrayed by the politicians who signed the peace treaty. It might even be argued that *every* nation lost in the war. An even stronger argument can be made that the war did not really end in 1918 but merely paused until 1939. That is the year in which what we now call World War II began.

Studying the War

UNDERSTANDING HISTORY involves much more than simply memorizing facts and dates. World War I had more battles than most people can name. All one really needs to know about most of those battles is that they had little impact on the course of the war as a whole. It is more important to know

what events were truly significant, *why* they happened as they did, and *how* they were connected with one another. As you read about the war, ask yourself these same what-why-how questions. Doing so will help you make sense of the war. And, as things begin making sense, the specific facts and dates will become easier to remember.

This introduction has raised questions about the kinds of changes World War I brought. Change is emphasized in every chapter. Another big question to think about is the American role in the war. While *World War I for Kids* covers all the main combatant nations, it pays special attention to aspects of the war in which the United States was involved. For this reason the book emphasizes events affecting western Europe, which is where the United States played its most important role.

Keep in mind that while the war lasted more than four years, Americans were fully involved in its fighting for barely a single year. Nevertheless, there is much to say about the US role as a *neutral* nation during the war's early years. It is therefore important to understand what it meant for a nation to be neutral. Truly neutral nations play no part in a war and favor neither side. Was the United States truly neutral before it joined with the Allies against the Central Powers in 1917? That is a question to think about while reading this book.

Another thing to do while studying the war is to pay close attention to maps. It is impossible to understand any war without knowing something about its geography. A single glance at a map of Europe, for example, helps explain why Great Britain had a powerful navy and a small army at the start of the war. As an island nation it always depended on ships to conduct its trade and needed a strong navy to protect it and to repel possible invaders. Another glance at the map helps explain why Russia and Turkey became enemies. Russia had ports on the Black Sea, but its ships sailing there could not reach the Mediterranean Sea and the wider world without passing through Turkey's Strait of Dardanelles that connects the Black and Mediterranean Seas. Other examples of the importance of geography are found throughout this book. Virtually every nation involved in the war had a unique geographical position that helped dictate the actions it took. The key geographical fact for the United States was its distance from Europe, which helps explain its long hesitation to get involved.

When the War Became "World War I"

THE EXPRESSION "World War I" was never used during the war itself. Through the war's early years, it was known simply as the "European War" because it involved mainly European nations. As it expanded into other regions, it became known as the "Great War" because of its unprecedented size. Eventually, it became known as "*the* World War" because it was being fought over a larger part of the world than any previous conflict in history. It was only after the outbreak of the second world war in 1939 that "the World War" took on a number to become World War I. The number was necessary to differentiate it from World War II.

1
THE ROAD TO WAR

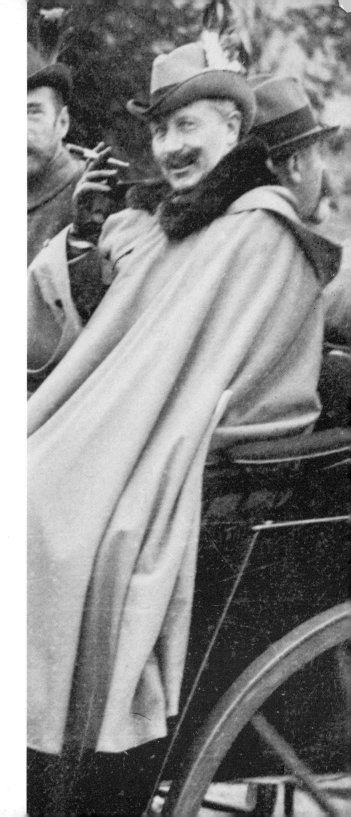

Understanding the "causes" of wars is rarely easy, and the reasons for the outbreak of World War I are especially difficult to comprehend even today. The outline of events leading up to the start of the war in 1914 is clear, but it is important to learn *why* these events occurred. Why did each nation involved in the war get into it? What did it expect to gain? What options did each nation have when it entered the war?

The first world war was complicated because the many nations fighting in it had very different reasons for doing so. Some nations, such as France and Belgium, had little choice because they were invaded and threatened with conquest. Others, such as Russia and Italy, might easily have stayed out. Some nations,

Archduke Franz Ferdinand with his family.

most notably Italy, could easily have fought on the side opposite to the one they joined. Even the United States, which eventually became an associated member of the Allied Powers in 1917, might conceivably have fought on the opposite side.

Europe in 1914

AS THE year 1914 opened, western Europe was enjoying unprecedented prosperity made possible by modern technological advances and more than four decades of general peace among the largest nations. Bloody conflicts had recently been fought in the Balkan region of southeastern Europe, and Russia had fought

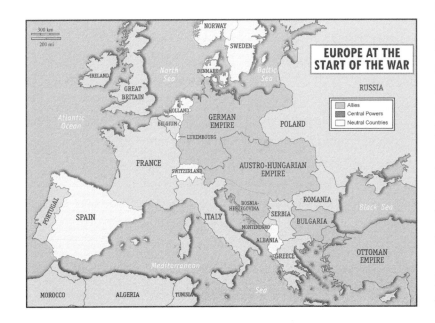

a war with Japan nearly a decade earlier, but those conflicts did not threaten the peace of western Europe. Great Britain, France, and Germany had fought many messy little wars against uprisings in their colonial territories, but those conflicts took place far from home and generally had little impact on European events. Because all these conflicts were far from western European power centers and were comparatively minor, few people in western Europe worried about the possibility of a bigger war that would affect them directly.

The last major war among western European nations had been the Franco-Prussian War of 1870. That conflict had lasted only about 10 months and had involved only two nations, but it indirectly contributed to the outbreak of World War I. Germany's crushing victory had taken the coal-rich Alsace-Lorraine border region from France and left the French bitterly resentful. By 1914, only the oldest French and German citizens remembered that war clearly. Nevertheless, France remained distrustful of Germany, and relations between the two neighboring countries were tense. Neither France nor Germany may have expected a new war, but both were prudent enough to prepare for that awful possibility.

Other wars among western European nations had been fought during the decades preceding the Franco-Prussian War, but most had been smaller conflicts involving only a few countries. The last truly continental conflicts engulfing western Europe had been fought from 1803 to 1815, when France's emperor Napoleon Bonaparte had tried to conquer all of Europe. He almost succeeded but was finally stopped by Great Britain. Those wars ended centuries of hostility between France and Great Britain and pitted most of Europe—including Russia—against France. At that time, neither Germany nor Italy had yet been unified, leaving Britain and Russia as the only powers strong enough to challenge France. As their battles were confined mostly to Europe, the Napoleonic Wars were not "world wars" in the same sense as the great 20th-century world wars. Nevertheless, they caused many deaths and changed the map of Europe. Britain's control of the seas and its decisive defeat of Napoleon at the Battle of Waterloo in 1815 ended those wars and ushered in a long era of comparative peace.

A century was a long time for Europe to go without a major war. That fact alone helped make Europeans feel confident that great wars would become relics of the past. Moreover, the 19th century proved to be an age of great industrial progress. It saw the development of powerful steam-driven machinery and engines, the spread of railroads, the harnessing of electricity, the rise of telegraphic and telephonic communications, and other great developments. By 1914, the world was thrilling to still more exciting inventions in aviation, automobile transportation, radio, and other fields. In the face of marvelous technological advances that increased industrial productivity and made human lives easier and more pleasant, it was only natural that people should think civilization was ready to put warfare behind it.

Europe's government and military leaders were prudent enough not to invest too much faith in wishful thinking and naive optimism. Europeans had seen too many wars in their history not to be wary of future wars. They kept their eyes on what neighboring nations were doing and made treaties (often secretly) with neighbors they could trust. Meanwhile, they quietly modernized their military forces and made contingency plans in case another major war should erupt.

No obvious signs of serious trouble appeared to be brewing on the Continent in 1914, aside from unsettled conflicts in the seemingly remote Balkan region, which encompassed Austrian-controlled Bosnia Herzegovina, independent Serbia, Bulgaria, Greece, and parts of the Turkish Ottoman Empire. The peoples of Britain, France, Italy, Belgium, the Netherlands, Germany, Austria-Hungary, and other western European countries had every reason to think their peace and prosperity would continue forever. With so much of western Europe prospering, what reason would any of its nations have for going to war?

AN ACCIDENTAL ASSASSINATION?

Gavrilo Princip, the 19-year-old Serbian who killed 51-year-old Archduke Franz Ferdinand, was a member of a radical Serbian nationalist organization known as the Black Hand. When that organization learned Ferdinand was coming to Bosnia's capital, Sarajevo, it assigned six men to kill him. At that time, Bosnia Herzegovina was the southernmost province of the Austro-Hungarian Empire. Its eastern neighbor, Serbia, was a small but independent nation. Because many ethnic Serbians lived in Bosnia, Serbian nationalists wanted to join Bosnia to a larger Serbian state. The Black Hand hoped to advance that goal by killing the heir to the Austro-Hungarian throne, even though Ferdinand himself was sympathetic to the ethnic minorities within the empire.

On June 28, 1914, Ferdinand and his wife, Sophie, arrived in Sarajevo and were slowly driven through the city in a small motorcade to the town hall. The Black Hand's six would-be assassins were stationed along the motorcade's route, quietly awaiting chances to strike. The plotters had had more than a month to prepare for that day, but things went wrong from the start. The first two men waiting to throw bombs at Ferdinand lost their nerve when his car went by them and did nothing. Minutes later, a third assassin tossed a bomb at Ferdinand's car, but it bounced off and exploded under the following car, injuring its passengers and many spectators. Ferdinand himself was unhurt.

Immediately after the bomb went off, the motorcade raced to the town hall. Along the way, Ferdinand's car passed two more assassins, including Princip, who did nothing. After reaching the town hall safely, Ferdinand delivered a little speech and then canceled the rest of his afternoon events so he could visit the men wounded by the bomb attack. On the way to the victims' hospital, Ferdinand's driver took a wrong turn. By sheer chance, he drove onto the very street where Princip was looking for something to eat after concluding that the assassination plot was off. The driver braked to turn around, and his car stalled close to where Princip was walking. When Princip suddenly saw Ferdinand sitting in the open car only a few yards away, he stepped closer and fired his revolver directly into him and into Sophie. He was arrested as the car sped away. Both Ferdinand and Sophie died before reaching a hospital. Princip himself later died in prison.

The history of the world might have been very different if Ferdinand had not elected to visit the hospital, if his driver had not made a wrong turn, or if Princip had gone elsewhere for lunch.

Almost immediately after shooting Archduke Ferdinand, Princip was seized by police, and his arrest was captured by a photographer.

Collection of the author

4

Trigger for War

UNFORTUNATELY, WARS sometimes do start unexpectedly and often without sensible reasons. That is essentially how World War I began. However, while all the reasons for the war may not be clear, the event that triggered it is. On June 28, 1914, an obscure young Serbian nationalist assassinated Archduke Franz Ferdinand, the heir to the Austro-Hungarian throne, in Bosnia. The assassination set in motion a sequence of events that would lead to war. It was a strange sequence, much like what happens when dominoes are lined up in rows on their edges: after one domino is tipped over, it knocks over a second domino, which in turn knocks over a third, and so on, until all the dominoes have fallen. World War I started because Ferdinand's assassination gave Austria-Hungary an excuse to wage war on tiny Serbia, tipping over the first of many dominoes.

From Provocation to War

ARCHDUKE FERDINAND'S assassination did not cause a great stir when the news reached western Europe. Western Europeans had grown used to hearing about conflicts in the Balkan region and did not immediately see how the assassination could affect them. Ferdinand had been the presumptive heir to the throne of Austria-Hungary, which traced its origins back to western Europe's great Holy Roman Empire. However, Austria-Hungary had become a tired, unwieldy empire that had lost the respect of its more powerful neighbors. Moreover, Ferdinand himself had not been well known outside his own country. Thus, while his assassination may have been regrettable, it did not seem like a calamitous event.

In central Europe, especially in Austria-Hungary, however, reactions were different. Franz Ferdinand had not been greatly liked by his uncle, Emperor Franz Joseph, or his government, but that did not matter. The assassination was seen as an act of rebellion threatening the integrity of the empire, which was already struggling to stay together. Austria-Hungary differed from Germany, France, Italy, and Great Britain, whose peoples shared common cultures. Austria-Hungary encompassed a patchwork of diverse cultures and nationalities with only its imperial government to bind them together. Forces starting to pull the empire apart were already at work. Those forces were strongest in its Balkan provinces, including Bosnia Herzegovina, where Ferdinand was killed.

Looking for someone to blame, Austria-Hungary accused independent Serbia of being behind Serbian disorders in Bosnia, including the assassination. It got ready to issue Serbia an ultimatum it expected would be rejected

Emperor Franz Joseph.

Russia's Tsar Nicholas II (left) and his cousin, Germany's Kaiser Wilhelm II (right), before the war.

and meanwhile prepared to invade that country. Its goal was to end ethnic unrest in its southern provinces so it could hold its empire together. Austria-Hungary figured that defeating tiny Serbia would be easy but had to take into account possible opposition from its huge eastern neighbor, Russia. Like the Serbians, Russians spoke a Slavic language, followed Eastern Orthodox Christianity, and shared other cultural similarities. Fearing that Russia would not idly watch a fellow Slavic nation be conquered, Austria-Hungary turned to its western neighbor, Germany, for support. This is where the origins of World War I become especially difficult to understand.

Germany had no special interests in the Balkans. It was not eager to go to war against Russia but probably expected it would eventually have to fight it. Germany had recently expanded and modernized its military forces. Its leaders seemed to think it would be wise to confront Russia right away, before Russia finished modernizing and training its own military. For that reason, its emperor, Kaiser Wilhelm II, promised military support to Austria-Hungary if it were attacked by Russia. Wilhelm was a first cousin of the Russian ruler, Tsar Nicholas II, and both were first cousins of Britain's King George V. Wilhelm figured his close personal relationship to Nicholas would delay any Russian military response to Germany's provocative action. At the same time, German leaders hoped Great Britain and France would not rush to get involved.

On July 23, 1914, Austria-Hungary presented Serbia with an ultimatum containing 10 specific demands. They included letting Austria-Hungary take part in Serbia's investigation of the assassination and the suppression of all anti-Austrian activities within Serbia. Austria-Hungary wanted an excuse to invade Serbia, so it worded its demands to ensure Serbia would reject them to avoid being humiliated. To the Austrians' surprise, however, Serbia quickly accepted all but a few minor points in the ultimatum. Nevertheless, Austria-Hungary declared war on Serbia on July 28—exactly one month after Ferdinand's assassination. The next day, Austrian troops began shelling Belgrade, the Serbian capital near the country's northern border with Austria-Hungary. Only two countries were involved, but World War I had begun.

Other Nations Join In

AFTER AUSTRIA-HUNGARY attacked Serbia, other nations began acting quickly. Russia was poorly governed and its military lacked modern equipment and training, but the country was so big and its army so large, it would be a formidable enemy merely because of its great size. When Russia began mobilizing its army on July 30, Germany responded by mobilizing its own military forces. The two countries' emperor cousins continued to communicate with each other constantly to cool things down, but on August 1, Germany declared war on Russia, France, and Belgium. Expecting that France would likely side with Russia, Germany then had to consider what to do about its equally dangerous western neighbor, which was still angry about the territory it had lost to Germany in 1870.

The possibility of Germany's going to war with France again was not a new idea in 1914. Eight years earlier, General Count Alfred von Schlieffen had devised a detailed plan for Germany to use should it find itself fighting both France and Russia. The so-called Schlieffen Plan called for Germany to invade and conquer France as quickly as possible, so it could then send its victorious troops east on trains to take on Russia before that country was completely ready to fight. Germany had the modern rail lines and railroad stock to move hundreds of thousands of troops east fast enough to make Schlieffen's daring plan work. However, to accomplish that feat, Germany could not afford to dicker with France. It had to act immediately, so it declared war on France on August 3.

Because France had heavily fortified the border it shared with Germany, the Schlieffen Plan called for German troops to enter France

PREWAR ALLIANCES

Through the years leading up to the war, western European nations were generally friendly toward one another. At the same time, however, undercurrents of distrust had created complex networks of defense treaties among the nations. Some treaties were secret—a practice that US president Woodrow Wilson would later say had helped cause the war.

One of the most important treaty groups was the Triple Alliance that had joined Germany, Austria-Hungary, and Italy in 1881. Conceived by Germany, it would become the basis for the Central Powers alliance during the war. A second major treaty group formed in opposition to it in 1907 was the Triple Entente. It joined Great Britain, France, and Russia and would become the basis for the wartime Allied Powers.

These major alliances required their members to support one another under certain specific wartime conditions. For example, terms of the Triple Alliance required Italy to back Germany if it were attacked by France. Because Germany eventually attacked France first, Italy was within its rights to stay out of the conflict. It later joined the Allied Powers. The same treaty required Germany and Austria-Hungary to back each other if either were attacked by Russia. Conditions in the Triple Entente treaty were less rigid. They merely suggested members had a "moral obligation" to back one another in case of war.

Meanwhile, all the major powers also signed additional treaties among themselves and with other nations. Some treaties were made public; others were kept secret. As one would imagine, as the first world war developed, leaders of the various nations paid close attention to what the treaties required other nations to do. France, for example, doubtless hesitated to attack Germany first, knowing that doing so would bring Italy into the war against it.

through its lightly defended northern borders with neutral Belgium and Luxembourg and then turn toward Paris and central France. Belgium was a comparatively weak country in which Germany had no particular interest, but

AMERICAN REACTIONS TO THE OUTBREAK OF WAR

Many Americans viewed the developing war in Europe with indifference or contempt. Unable to understand why the Continent's leading nations wanted to fight one another, they regarded the war as another example of the Old World's backward thinking and were glad not to be involved. This, however, did not prevent individual Americans from choosing sides in the war.

On August 4, US president Woodrow Wilson proclaimed that the United States would remain neutral in the new war. Fifteen days later, he addressed Congress, calling for a policy of strict neutrality. His administration would maintain that policy until early 1917.

In his speech, President Wilson said the following:

> The effect of the war upon the United States will depend upon what American citizens say and do. Every man who really loves America will act and speak in the true spirit of neutrality, which is the spirit of impartiality and fairness and friendliness to all concerned....
>
> The people of the United States are drawn from many nations, and chiefly from the nations now at war. It is natural and inevitable that there should be the utmost variety of sympathy and desire among them with regard to the issues and circumstances of the conflict.
>
> Some will wish one nation, others another, to succeed in the momentous struggle. It will be easy to excite passion and difficult to allay it. Those responsible for exciting it will assume a heavy responsibility, responsibility for no less a thing than that the people of the United States, whose love of their country and whose loyalty to its government should unite them as Americans all....
>
> I venture, therefore, my fellow countrymen, to speak a solemn word of warning to you against that deepest, most subtle, most essential breach of neutrality which may spring out of partisanship, out of passionately taking sides.
>
> The United States must be neutral in fact, as well as in name, during these days that are to try men's souls.

Women were among the leaders in pushing for peace. In early 1915, 1,200 delegates to the International Congress of Women in the Netherlands discussed ways to end the war. The American delegation (pictured here) included Jane Addams (second from left), who in 1931 would become the first American woman to win a Nobel Peace Prize.

Library of Congress LC-DIG-ggbain-18848

because a speedy conquest of France was essential, Germany launched its invasion in Belgium.

Germany's attack on Belgium quickly brought Great Britain into the war. Britain had a treaty with Belgium guaranteeing it would help defend its neutrality against invasion. Germany had also guaranteed Belgian neutrality, but that guarantee now meant nothing. While Britain was obligated to defend Belgium, it also had its own issues with Germany. In recent years, Germany had been building up its modern navy with the obvious intent of challenging British naval dominance in the world. Germany was envious of Britain's vast colonial empire throughout Africa, Asia, and parts of the Americas. The British naturally felt threatened by Germany, so they had their own motives for reducing German military power.

On August 4, Britain declared war against Germany. This was bad news for Germany. Despite Germany's great naval buildup, it was not quite ready to take on Russia, France, and Britain all at once. Its first priority was now clearer than ever. It had to defeat France with its army before British troops could play a role, and then move against Russia. As Germany began invading Belgium, it expected to easily brush aside that country's small military forces and advance quickly into France. The Belgians, however, had other ideas, and Germany's Schlieffen Plan was soon in trouble.

Make a Military Recruiting Poster

EVERY NATION FIGHTING in the war advertised to recruit soldiers and sailors. In the days before television and radio, posters were one of the most effective means of reaching the public. Governments used skilled writers to compose persuasive appeals along with snappy slogans. Professional artists added eye-catching illustrations. The posters of different countries reflected cultural differences but generally appealed to the same basic emotions—patriotism, pride, fear, desire for revenge, shame, thirst for glory, and desire to learn new skills. Your challenge is to design an original recruiting poster for World War I.

Materials
- ✪ Note paper
- ✪ Pen or pencil
- ✪ Poster-size paper
- ✪ Drawing and painting tools
- ✪ Computer connected to Internet and printer
- ✪ Scissors
- ✪ Glue or paste for paper

Begin by jotting down ideas. Decide what country your post-

er is for. Is it for one armed service or military specialty, or for all the country's services? What type of appeal do you wish to make? Anger toward the enemy? Fear of enemy invasion? Simple pride in patriotism and desire to serve? Your choices will help direct the wording of your poster and the kinds of illustrations that work best.

If you like to draw, you can illustrate your poster yourself. If not, you can find appropriate illustrations on the Internet, print them, cut them out, and paste them to your poster. Draw or look for pictures of flags, uniformed servicemen, political and military leaders, warships, airplanes, tanks, and symbols such as the Statue of Liberty, Eiffel Tower, or Berlin's Brandenburg Gate.

Immediately after Britain declared war on Germany, it campaigned to get men to volunteer for the military with simple appeals from its greatest living war hero, Horatio Herbert Kitchener.

Library of Congress LC-USZ62-109369

2

STALEMATE ON THE WESTERN FRONT

THROUGHOUT THE HISTORY of great European wars, huge armies had traditionally swept into enemy territories hoping to overwhelm resistance through the speed and weight of their forces. This is exactly what the Schlieffen Plan called for the German army to do against Belgium and France. The plan had been worked out in such detail it even contained a precise schedule of when each invasion step should occur. A key element of the plan was for the right flank of the German army to sweep so far to the west that its last soldier could touch the sea. This naturally meant the Germans would have to advance far into Belgium.

Kaiser Wilhelm II (right) inspecting German troops at the start of the war.

Conquest of Belgium

ON AUGUST 2, 1914, Germany sent its first troops into Luxembourg, which was so small and weak it scarcely counted in the war. Meanwhile, the government gave Belgium 12 hours to accept its demand for free passage through that country. The next day, as Germany declared war on France, Belgium rejected its demands and appealed to Great Britain for help. Britain immediately began to mobilize. On August 4, as German troops entered Belgium, Britain declared war on Germany.

Although the Belgians refused to capitulate, they knew as well as the Germans did that they had no chance of repelling the invasion. Their army put up a strong resistance, and even Belgian civilians shot at the advancing Germans. Civilian involvement in fighting went against accepted wartime practices. The Germans responded by executing many Belgian civilians—including women and children—and

Belgian family sleeping in a barn while fleeing from German occupation of their homeland.

Liberty's Victorious Conflict: A Photographic History of the World War (Chicago: Magazine Circulation Co., 1918)

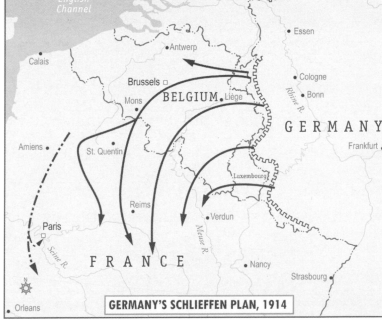

GERMANY'S SCHLIEFFEN PLAN, 1914

burning whole towns to the ground. These actions naturally aroused outside opinion against Germany and laid a basis for Allied propaganda denouncing Germans as barbaric "Huns." Germany's later unnecessary destruction of a great medieval library in the city of Liège stood in sharp contrast to Germany's treasured self-image as a center of higher culture.

The Germans greatly underestimated the Belgian resolve. Strengthened by the courageous example of their king, Albert I, Belgian troops were ready to die rather than surrender. In addition to meeting stronger resistance from Belgian troops than expected, the German advance was slowed by having to knock out a string of strong fortresses protecting the east Belgian city of Liège. When huge artillery weapons failed to reduce Liège's main citadel, the German commander, Major General Erich von Ludendorff, called for a zeppelin airship to drop bombs on Liège. This first use of an aircraft as a bombing weapon did little damage. It did, however, herald a future trend in which aerial bombing would bring the horror of war ever closer to civilian populations. Meanwhile, Ludendorff finally broke open the Belgian fortresses with a giant howitzer cannon, nicknamed "Big Bertha," whose shells could penetrate thick concrete walls.

As German troops completed their conquest of Belgium over the next two weeks, other

EDITH CAVELL

Germany's invasion of Belgium badly damaged its reputation among neutral countries, especially the United States. Its reputation suffered a second blow when it executed a British nurse named Edith Cavell who had been working in Belgium. For almost a year, the 49-year-old Cavell had helped Allied soldiers escape from German-occupied Belgium, nearly 200 in all. In August 1915, she was arrested and charged with treason under German law. The fact that she freely admitted exactly what she had done made it easy for a court-martial to convict her, and she was sentenced to be executed. During the two months she was under arrest, her case excited worldwide protests. The United States was among the nations pressuring Germany not to execute her. Nevertheless, on October 12, 1915, she was shot by a firing squad. Her patriotism and courage up to the moment of her death made her a powerful martyr symbol throughout the remainder of the war.

Her last message before dying was "Patriotism is not enough."

Although Cavell was punished under German law, Germany was well within its Geneva Convention rights to execute her. The convention, which governed countries' behavior while at war, normally protected medical personnel. However, Cavell had lost that protection when she used her medical work as a cover to aid soldiers who were enemies of Germany. Nevertheless, many nations regarded her execution as a war crime, and world opinion remained strongly against Germany. The Allies, especially Britain, used Cavell in their propaganda to depict Germany as a nation so barbaric it killed women who nursed Germany's own wounded soldiers. Along with Germany's occupation of Belgium and sinking of the passenger liner *Lusitania* (see chapter 6), Cavell's execution contributed to the later decisions of the United States and other neutral nations to enter the war against Germany.

Belgian king Albert (left) and French general
Ferdinand Foch at the front.

would not last more than a few months. By the end of August 1914, that optimistic assessment was looking doubtful.

The War Moves into France

AFTER BELGIUM finally fell to the Germans, the invasion force turned its full strength to the south against France on August 23. By that time, British army units were in position to support the French defense. Under heavy bombardment from German long-range artillery fire, the Allies spent two weeks slowly retreating a little more than 100 miles south of the border, to the Marne River, which joins the Seine at Paris. Fighting fiercely the entire way, they made the Germans work hard for every inch of ground they gained.

On September 5, 1914, the first and perhaps most important of the many great battles that would be fought along the western front began. Over the next five days, more than two million troops—almost evenly divided between Germans and Allies—fought. The stakes in what became known as the First Battle of the Marne were enormous. The Allies were fighting to save France's capital from conquest, and the Germans were fighting to make their grand war plan succeed. The French government evacuated the capital, leaving it in the hands of the military. If Paris fell to the Germans, it

units began advancing into northern France. Meanwhile, Russia was advancing on Germany from the east much more quickly than had been anticipated. Developments on the eastern front intensified German urgency in conquering France on the western front, and Germany was forced to divert troops from the west to the east much sooner than it had intended. German troops were winning battles against the Russians in the east, but every delay in the west made the eastern situation more perilous. When the war began, Germany expected it

was likely that the rest of the country would soon follow.

Although the Battle of the Marne took place barely one month after the war had begun, it proved to be a crucial turning point. The Allies exploited gaps in the enemy positions that enabled them to stop the German advance. They thereby saved not only Paris but perhaps the entire country. Some historians think the battle cost Germany its best chance to win the war.

Failure of the Schlieffen Plan

AFTER STOPPING the German advance, the Allies pushed the exhausted German troops nearly halfway back to the northern border. The German retreat stopped near the Aisne River. There the Germans dug long lines of trenches and settled in. Being closer to their supply lines to the north made it easier for them to maintain their position there. One of the reasons their

French refugee children waiting to be transported away from the fighting.

National Archives and Records Administration

TAXI CABS TO THE RESCUE

One of the most colorful stories to come out of the war concerns the First Battle of the Marne. As German troops were closing in on Paris, the French did not have enough military vehicles to transport reserve troops to a weak point in the city's defenses. A crisis was averted when Paris's military governor had the city's civilian taxis gathered together. Under his direction, about 600 taxis shuttled more than 4,000 badly needed troops to the front. Their arrival helped turn the tide against the Germans. On the 50th anniversary of the battle in 1964, France issued a postage stamp commemorating the taxis' contribution to the Allied victory.

Collection of Richard Countess

drive on Paris had failed had been the inability of German supply lines and reserve troops to keep up with the long advance.

Despite eight years of careful planning, Germany's grand Schlieffen Plan had clearly failed when its armies were turned back at the Marne. Instead of quickly knocking France out of the war so it could send its troops east to finish off the Russians, Germany found itself mired in a two-front war. This failure demonstrated the folly of depending on an elaborate plan that cannot take into account unpredictable events. Mistakes were made by the German commanders, including General Helmuth von Moltke, who modified the overall plan, but the Germans were also handicapped by several unexpected developments. One was having to divert troops to the Russian front sooner than had been expected. Another was having British troops come to France's aid. Germany had not expected Britain to enter the war—at least not so soon.

No one would have guessed it at the time, but the Aisne would remain the main German position on the western front for nearly four years as the fighting on the western front became deadlocked. Modern warfare had changed in ways that leaders of all the armies would need time to figure out. Meanwhile, however, the Germans would continue to press into France—without much success, but

with devastating consequences for both sides in the war. While the German armies recuperated from their ordeal in their new trenches and their leaders planned new strategies, fighting continued on the eastern front, and Britain and Germany launched a naval war that would extend the fighting to regions far beyond Europe. Those sectors of the war are the subjects of later chapters.

Deadlock on the Western Front

THROUGH THE next four years, the Germans and the Allies continuously struggled to find ways to break the deadlock in which their armies were becoming stuck. Periodically, one side or the other would mount a major offensive, throw a large force against an enemy position, and then watch its troops being slaughtered while making little or no progress. General Joseph Joffre, who commanded the French army at the start of the war, demanded constant offensive fighting. "Every effort must be made to attack and drive back the enemy," he ordered. "A soldier who can no longer advance must guard the territory already held, no matter what the cost. He must be killed where he stands rather than draw back." The consequence of such orders was generally thousands of dead French soldiers with little or nothing to show for their sacrifices. During those four years, millions

Write a Poem About the War

THE RANKS OF the British army produced a number of exceptional poets who left elegant poetic records of their wartime experiences. Many of them died during World War I and consequently never knew their poetry would make their names famous. One of the finest of these poets was Wilfred Owen, a young English teacher who enlisted in an army unit in the fall of 1915. After completing his training, he was commissioned an officer and posted to France. There he served in the trenches and suffered through several heavy bombardments that led to his hospitalization. While convalescing from shell shock in England he was befriended by the poet Siegfried Sassoon, who encouraged him to record his experiences in poetry. His most famous poem, "Dulce et Decorum Est," captures both the horrors of the western front and the hypocrisy of claiming that dying for one's country in battle is "*dulce et decorum*" (sweet and glorious).

After returning to France in 1918, Owen distinguished himself in combat but was killed in action on November 4—exactly one week before the armistice that ended the fighting.

Wilfred Owen.

Wilfred Owen, *Poems* (1920)

He was only 25 years old. After the war, he was posthumously awarded a Military Cross, and Sassoon arranged for publication of his poems.

Dulce et Decorum Est

Bent double, like old beggars under sacks,
Knock-kneed, coughing like hags, we cursed
*   through sludge,*
Till on the haunting flares we turned our backs
And towards our distant rest began to trudge.
Men marched asleep. Many had lost their boots
But limped on, blood-shod. All went lame; all blind;
Drunk with fatigue; deaf even to the hoots
Of disappointed shells that dropped behind.

GAS! Gas! Quick, boys!—An ecstasy of fumbling,
Fitting the clumsy helmets just in time;
But someone still was yelling out and stumbling
And floundering like a man in fire or lime.—
Dim, through the misty panes and thick green light
As under a green sea, I saw him drowning.

In all my dreams, before my helpless sight,
He plunges at me, guttering, choking, drowning.

If in some smothering dreams you too could pace
Behind the wagon that we flung him in,
And watch the white eyes writhing in his face,
His hanging face, like a devil's sick of sin;
If you could hear, at every jolt, the blood
Come gargling from the froth-corrupted lungs,

Obscene as cancer, bitter as the cud
Of vile, incurable sores on innocent tongues,—
My friend, you would not tell with such high zest
To children ardent for some desperate glory,
The old Lie: Dulce et decorum est
Pro patria mori.

Materials

✪ Writing or printing paper
✪ Pencil, pen, or computer word processor

Owen's poem is a personal remembrance of seeing soldiers die in combat. Its last line is a Latin phrase that translates as "it is sweet and seemly to die for one's country." The poem shows why that sentiment is a lie.

Try to imagine yourself experiencing some of the things that men and women did during the war—such as fighting in the trenches, piloting airplanes, serving on submarines, nursing wounded soldiers, training animals, or anything else that captures your imagination. When you find a subject that moves you, write a poem about it from the point of view of a person experiencing it first-hand in the war.

Poetry can take many forms. Its verses often follow fixed rhyming patterns, but unrhymed free verse can be equally poetical. Whether you use rhymes or not, try to build rhythms that reinforce the message of your poem.

of bullets and millions of artillery shells were fired and millions of soldiers were wounded or killed, but the main battle lines barely budged.

European wars of the past had been wars of movement, with vast armies sweeping over hundreds of miles. World War I was very different. New technologies and weapons had made it easier for armies to hold strong defensive positions. It would take a little longer to develop offensive weapons to overcome the defenses' advantages. In the meantime, armies going on the attack could barely move.

The weapon that had the most striking impact on ground fighting early in the war was the machine gun. Machine guns were not a new weapon, but the models used in 1914 fired so much faster and more accurately than earlier models that the armies of both sides did not immediately know how to deal with them. Whenever units of soldiers tried to cross open ground, it was easy for enemy forces simply to mow them down with intense machine gun fire. Firearms of all types had become more accurate and easier to fire quickly and were therefore more dangerous than weapons of the past. The best way for foot soldiers to protect themselves from being shot was to avoid moving above the surface of the ground—especially in open fields. This is precisely why troops on both sides literally "dug in." By the end of 1914, most German and Allied soldiers

on the frontlines were spending much of their time in trenches deep enough to keep their heads below ground level.

Another crucial change in weaponry was the development of artillery guns that could fire farther, faster, and more accurately than artillery of the past. Moreover, these new weapons could fire enormous shells loaded with explosive charges. When the combatants launched new offensives, they typically used their big guns to pound enemy positions for days, sometimes weeks, before sending their troops forward. Like the machine guns, the artillery weapons encouraged armies to dig in ever deeper. Sometimes artillery barrages that rained thousands of tons of shells on enemy positions proved ineffective because the enemies had dug in so deeply the shells did not hurt them. This kind of fighting further limited troop movements, thereby contributing to the general lack of mobility on the battlefields.

Another even simpler development restricting troop movement was the heavy use of barbed wire around defensive positions. A 19th-century American invention that ranchers used for fencing to control their herds, barbed wire was extensively used by all sides in World War I. Attacking soldiers could not easily get through coils of wire strung around defensive positions even if they carried wire cutters, and they could be painfully injured if they tried.

For all these reasons and others, the contest on the western front became what is called a war of attrition. In that kind of war, clear battlefield victories are rare and military leaders try to wear down their enemies until they collapse or give up in exhaustion before their own forces do the same. Soon, it seemed likely that the losing side on the western front would be the first one to run out of fresh troops, food, or military supplies. After a few years, both sides were running short on everything.

Italy Enters the War

THROUGH THE rest of 1914, the western front remained relatively quiet as both sides dug in their defensive positions and considered what to do next. In early 1915, Britain drew Italy into the Allied orbit. Although Italy had been one of the principal members of the prewar Triple Alliance, it had insisted on remaining neutral when Germany and Austria-Hungary went to war. By early 1915, the Italians sensed they could add to their territory by entering the war. They asked Austria-Hungary to concede some of its southern territories in exchange for Italy's joining the Central Powers. After the Austrians declined their offer, they turned to the British.

The British offered Italy portions of Austria-Hungary, Albania, Turkey, and even North Africa in return for its joining the Allies. Britain

CHRISTMAS ON THE WESTERN FRONT

When the war began in August, leaders of both sides confidently predicted it would end in time for troops to be home by Christmas. After several months of fighting, however, it was clear that would not happen. Seesaw battles continued into late December, when the western front started to quiet down. As Christmas Day arrived, many soldiers on both sides voluntarily laid down their weapons. Christmas, they felt, was a day for celebrating and reflecting, not for killing. Throughout the day, undeclared truces prevailed over many war zones, but fighting did occur in some.

In some sectors British and German soldiers carried their truces even further. As the sun rose near Ypres in Belgium that day, British soldiers huddling in their trenches heard German Christmas carols wafting across the no-man's-land separating them from the Germans. Then they saw lighted Christmas trees—which had been invented in Germany—rising from enemy trenches. When it was evident no one would shoot at them, German soldiers ventured out into no-man's-land, shouting Christmas greetings to the British and

offering to share their cigarettes and drinks. Some British soldiers even produced soccer balls and kicked them around with the Germans. A British officer who witnessed the enemy troops mingling together said, "It was absolutely astounding, and if I had seen it on a cinematograph film I should have sworn that it was faked."

Mingling among enemy soldiers and wandering about safely above ground were welcome contrasts to what the soldiers on both sides had experienced during the months leading up to Christmas. This would, however, be the last time large numbers of enemy soldiers met each other on such friendly terms. Their commanders issued orders forbidding fraternizing with enemies. The war would last four more years, and the same soldiers would face each other in many future battles. Nevertheless, the attitude of common soldiers toward their enemy counterparts would remain generally friendly and respectful when they were not actually fighting. To them, enemy soldiers were simply ordinary, working-class men who, like themselves, had been badly used by their countries' upper classes.

controlled none of those territories but had nothing to lose by making the offer. On April 26, 1915, Italy signed a secret pact with Britain. A month later, it declared war on Austria-Hungary. Soon afterward, it launched an offensive against its northern neighbor through the rugged Tyrolean Alps.

Italy's entrance into the war opened a new front between northern Italy and Austro-Hungarian territory. The Allies hoped that having to fight Italy would draw Central Powers forces away from the western front in northern France. Meanwhile, the Italians and Austro-Hungarians waged fierce battles in mountainous terrain that were very different from the fighting in other sectors of the war. Both sides suffered heavy losses with neither side making substantial gains. As on the western front, the Italian-Austro-Hungarian front degenerated into a stalemate. Italy had a large army, but it was poorly equipped and not well led. It would enjoy few victories during the war.

Renewed Fighting on the Western Front

AFTER UNPRODUCTIVE but bloody fighting through 1915, the next great battle on the western front was fought at the old French fortress town of Verdun, about 175 miles east of Paris, whose eastern approaches it guarded.

The strategic importance of the town was no longer great. Because of Verdun's symbolic significance in French history, however, the Germans expected the French to divert so many troops and resources defending it they would weaken their war effort. Germany's main goal was to make Verdun such a drain on French resources that Germany could break the stalemate on the western front.

On February 21, 1916, Germany began its offensive against Verdun with an artillery barrage from 1,400 guns that fired more than 100,000 shells per hour throughout the first day. Amazingly, most of the town's defenders survived the barrage. Even more amazingly, the ensuing battle lasted 10 months. On December 18, the Germans finally gave up and withdrew. By then, the French had lost nearly 350,000 men. However, the Germans lost almost as many themselves, so the balance of forces remained about the same as it had been at the start. Neither side had anything to show for its sacrifices in the long Battle of Verdun. One thing that did come out of the battle was that Henri-Philippe Pétain, the French general leading the defense of Verdun, emerged as a national hero. In 1918, he would become commander in chief of all French forces.

While the Battle of Verdun was still going on, another great battle was fought farther to the west. In July, the Allies launched their own major offensive against the Germans along the Somme River, northwest of Paris. Because the French had sent so many of their army divisions to protect Verdun, the British took the lead in what became known as the First Battle of the Somme. After an artillery bombardment of German positions lasting eight days, the Allied offensive began on July 1. As was the case in most western front battles, both sides suffered heavy losses with little to show for them. One of the main effects of the battle was to devastate the ranks of experienced German junior and noncommissioned officers. German forces would not recover from these losses throughout the rest of the war.

The First Battle of the Somme lasted into November and ended indecisively. On its first day alone, the British lost 58,000 men, one-third of whom were killed. It was the worst casualty toll for one day in British history. The long battle's total casualty figures were even greater than those of Verdun. Altogether, the British lost about 420,000 men, the French about 200,000, and the Germans about 500,000. In the time since the war ended, the Somme's name has come to symbolize the tragic waste of human lives in World War I.

Verdun and the Somme were merely the largest and most prolonged of numerous battles waged along the western front from 1915 through 1916. Like those epic battles, the smaller battles were generally characterized by high casualty tolls and minor gains by either side. Through those years, the stalemate conditions on the western front continued, and few people realized how long it would take to break the stalemate. A British officer writing home to his mother from the western front made a prophetic remark: "People out here seem to think that the war is going to be quite short. Why, I don't know; personally, I see nothing to prevent it going on forever."

There were, however, signs of coming changes in the way the war was fought. Aerial combat was becoming important and would have an impact on the ground fighting. Meanwhile, an important new ground weapon appeared for the first time in history.

In mid-September 1916, the British introduced the first tanks at Somme. Propelled by caterpillar-type tracks instead of wheels, these armored vehicles were merely lumbering curiosities on their first appearance in battle. But they held out the promise of upsetting the conditions of trench warfare and possibly helping to break the long stalemate. It would, however, take another year for tanks to become effective.

3

TRENCH WARFARE

W HEN PEOPLE THINK about World War I, the first images likely to spring to their minds are weary, mud-covered soldiers in tin helmets languishing in filthy trenches on the western front. Most soldiers serving in western Europe did spend time in trenches, but the trench conditions did not prevail everywhere, even along the western front. Trenches had been used in earlier wars and would also be used in later wars, but never to the extent they were employed in World War I, which truly was the classic example of "trench warfare." Why this was so has much to do with technological changes that made the war as a whole unique in history.

This museum model of a trench system provides a clearer picture of how the lines of trenches were constructed. Note the zigzag patterns, the connecting lines, and the holes made by artillery shells.

The essential reason trenches were used was simple: they helped prevent soldiers from being shot. Why trenches were used much more in World War I than in earlier conflicts also has a simple explanation: the guns used in that war could be fired faster, more accurately, and over greater distances than the weapons of earlier wars. In other words, World War I soldiers exposed on open ground were much more likely to be shot than soldiers of earlier eras. When soldiers had no trees, walls, or other solid barriers for protection, they found the best way to avoid being shot was to go underground. To do that, they dug trenches deep enough to keep their heads below ground level even when they were standing upright.

Trenches were used in all the European fronts. They reached their most elaborate and most extensive forms along the western front, where the general stalemate prevented all the armies from moving far from their bases.

Trench Warfare Begins on the Western Front

WHEN THE war began on the western front, both sides expected it to be a war of movement, with vast armies marching forward and backward over great distances, as in wars of the past. That expectation faded after the First Battle of the Marne, in which Germany's advance into northern France was turned back. That battle had demonstrated the futility of sending waves of cavalry and infantry in headlong assaults on the enemy, only to be mown down by modern rifle and machine gun fire.

After the Germans had retreated about halfway back to France's northern border, they stopped and decided to build strong defensive positions where they were. After selecting the most favorable locations, usually on high

General Front Line, December 1914–June 1918
Armistice Line, November 11, 1918

HOLLAND

• Utrecht
• Arnhem

English Channel

Ems R.

25 km
25 mi

• Essen
• Antwerp

Calais

□ Brussels
Liège •

• Cologne
• Bonn

Rhine R.

Mons •

BELGIUM

GERMANY

St. Quentin •

Amiens •

Frankfurt •

Luxembourg •

Reims •

Verdun •

Paris
□

Meuse R.

Seine R.

FRANCE

Nancy •

Strasbourg

• Orleans

WESTERN FRONT, 1914–1918

ground, they dug trenches deep enough to keep their soldiers out of direct enemy fire, set up their own machine guns and artillery, and waited for the Allies to attack them. The Germans expected to use their first trenches for only a few months at most. That was another miscalculation. They would actually continue to use those original trenches for four years. Meanwhile, the Allies starting building their own trench systems south of the German line, and trench warfare was born.

Eventually, German and Allied lines of trenches would stretch, almost without a break, from France's border with Switzerland to the North Sea—a distance of about 475 miles. The trench lines themselves were never straight, and most trench systems, on both sides, had at least three parallel lines. The total length of all trenches on the western front could have been as much as 15,000 miles. Digging all those trenches required tools. By the end of the war, the British army alone had issued more than 10 million shovels to troops on all the fronts.

Physical Characteristics of the Trenches

STRETCHING HUNDREDS of miles, the trenches cut through a wide variety of terrain—from flat, boggy lowlands near the coast to rocky highlands farther inland. As physical conditions varied in different regions, so, too, did the trench systems. In general, the Germans held higher positions because they selected their sites first. In combat, higher ground is always better than lower ground because it is easier to see what enemy forces are doing when looking down on them than it is when looking up. And, thanks to the law of gravity, it is easier to fire and hurl weapons down than up.

Holding the higher ground gave the Germans not only a tactical advantage over Allies positioned below them but also more livable conditions within their trenches. Many of the Allied trenches, especially toward the coast regions, were close to underground water tables and consequently were impossible to keep dry. Moisture posed major health risks to soldiers who had trouble keeping their feet dry in damp trenches. Soldiers whose feet remained cold and wet for days at a time often contracted trench foot. This painful condition, which took its name from the war's trench conditions, is similar to frostbite and can have the same nasty consequences, including amputation. It afflicted many Allied soldiers during the war, adding to their general misery. A Scottish army officer wrote, "No one who was not there can fully appreciate the excruciating agonies and misery through which the men had to go.... Paddling about by day, sometimes with water above their knees; standing at night, hour after hour on sentry duty, while the drenched boots, puttees and breeches became stiff like cardboard with ice from the freezing cold air." Moisture in the trenches also fostered other problems by making it easier for vermin such as body lice, insects, and rats to breed.

Trench Designs

TRENCHES WERE never laid out in long, straight lines. This was partly because they had to follow the changing natural terrain. Even when they were laid out in flatlands, however, they were never straight. They were designed either in zigzag patterns or in crenelated lines, like the battlements of medieval castles, to make them safer when they were under enemy attack. The reason for this should be self-evident: If soldiers in a trench were all visible in one long line, a single enemy machine gun could be fired down the trench and conceivably hit every single soldier. In a zigzag or crenelated trench, a machine gun could fire at a distance of only a few yards. Irregular lines also limited the effects of artillery shells that exploded in trenches.

Trench layouts had other complications, too. For example, many had narrow passageways extending as far as 30 yards in front of their main lines, with little observation posts known as saps. The saps were big enough for two or three soldiers to watch and listen for approaching enemies. All trench systems also had extensions for the latrines, or toilets, that soldiers needed to relieve themselves.

Trenches were usually dug in three parallel rows. The forward trenches held the soldiers actively involved in fighting. These were the trenches from which they went "over the top" into no-man's-land when advancing on enemy positions. The second line of trenches contained the support lines, from which ammunition and supplies were moved to the front. The third lines housed reserve soldiers, who were held back from fighting until they were absolutely needed. All the lines were connected by passages cut between them. German trench systems were the most highly developed. Some had as many as 10 lines.

Trenches also varied greatly in depth, size, design, and other details. Most trenches were deep enough for their occupants to move around with their heads below ground level, out of sight of enemy guns. All trenches had raised areas called fire steps on which soldiers stood when they fired their rifles over the parapets (top edges) of the trenches.

The dugouts in the supply and reserve trenches behind the frontlines tended to be much deeper than those of frontline trenches because they were bombarded more heavily by enemy artillery fire. Some dugouts were as

French soldiers using a large box periscope to peer over the top of their trench.

Make a Periscope

FACED WITH THE ever-present danger of being shot if they poked their heads above their trenches, soldiers needed safe ways to see what was going on outside. One solution was to use periscopes to peer over the top. Best known as the viewing devices submarine crews used to see what was happening above the water, periscopes are rectangular or tubular viewing instruments that use mirrors to see over or around obstacles. Light entering a lens or opening at the top reflects off a prism or mirror straight down to a second prism or mirror that reflects it out a second opening into the viewer's eyes.

World War I soldiers used periscopes not only to see over the tops of their trenches but sometimes also to aim their rifles without having to expose themselves to enemy fire. You can make a simple mirror periscope with ordinary household items and use it to experience the feeling of peering over the top of a trench.

Materials

✪ 2 one-quart cardboard milk cartons

✪ Scissors

✪ 2 small rectangular pocket mirrors that fit within the cartons (if you do not have suitable mirrors at home, buy square mirrors about 2¾ inches wide at a craft store)

✪ Adhesive tape

In this activity you will make two identical parts of a periscope that you will join together. Start by cutting the tops off two milk cartons. Wash out the cartons and dry them. Cut a square opening at the bottom of one side of each carton, leaving a border about ¼ inch wide around its edges. Use tape to attach a rectangular mirror inside each opening you have cut, placing it, glass side up, at

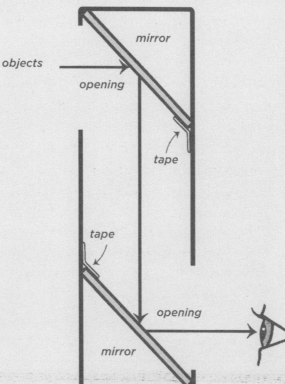

a 45-degree angle. When you hold each carton at eye level and look inside its opening at the mirror, you should see what is directly above the carton. Adjust the mirror as necessary to correct its position, then use enough tape to hold it firmly in place when the carton is turned upside down. The final step is to connect the two cartons. Place one carton upright on a firm surface with its opening facing you. Turn the other carton upside down with its opening facing away from you. Pinch in its sides just enough to slide it into the top of the first carton, and then tape the two cartons together.

If the only mirrors you can find are too large for 1-quart cartons, try using 2-quart cartons or cardboard boxes of suitable sizes. When you are done with your periscope, you can return the mirrors to their original uses.

German officers enjoying the relative comfort of their well-constructed trenches.

Collier's New Photographic History of the World's War (New York: P. F. Collier & Son, 1918)

deep as 30 or 40 feet underground. Frontline trenches were bombarded less frequently because of the danger of artillery shells falling on the enemy's own frontline trenches, which were often only a stone's throw away.

The quarters in which soldiers slept and sheltered themselves from the weather varied greatly. The dugout shelters in many frontline trenches on both sides were little more than crude lean-to structures, protected from weather and enemy bombardment only by corrugated iron, boards, or logs. Shelters in German backline trenches were dug deep underground and provided spacious rooms, often with comfortable furniture. Some officer quarters even had whitewashed ceilings, carpeting, and glass windows.

Conditions in Allied trenches tended to be far more primitive, especially in areas where underground water was always a problem. The floors of many trenches were constantly muddy, if not submerged in water. Boardwalks were constructed in many trenches to allow soldiers to walk on dry surfaces. To combat the problem of eroding dirt walls, the walls of the trenches were often reinforced with stacks of sandbags or wood pilings, especially below the parapets facing enemy lines. The Germans built concrete walls in many of their trenches.

Not surprisingly, the atmosphere inside frontline trenches, and especially inside their dugouts, was generally dank and even fetid, and vermin were a constant problem. These conditions were naturally unhealthy, but troops were generally rotated through the frontlines frequently enough to avoid large-scale health problems.

No-Man's-Land and Other Hazards

IN MANY western front sectors the frontline trenches of opposing armies were separated from each other by an average of about 150 yards—the length of one and a half football fields. Some were closer than 50 yards from each other and others as far away as 500 yards. The space between any two enemy trenches was known as "no-man's-land." Because neither side controlled it, it was literally no man's land.

The no-man's-land areas were generally the most dangerous pieces of land in war zones. Hidden snipers were constantly on the lookout for enemy soldiers to shoot. Any soldier who raised his head above the parapet of his trench or stepped out onto no-man's-land was likely to be shot at almost instantly. When waves of soldiers were ordered to go "over the top" to advance on enemy positions, they were likely to encounter immediate barrages of machine gun fire. Many, perhaps most, of the trench soldiers killed along the western front died in no-man's-land areas. Going over the top was terrifying, but waiting to go could be almost as bad, according to an American Marine corporal: "That waiting around before you go over always gets my goat. Gee it makes me nervous. After I get started it is different, but that waiting around sure gets on a guy's nerves. It makes your mouth dry. Everybody kept asking, 'What time is it?' They would ask it a thousand times."

Soldiers who managed to cross no-man's-land without being shot during assaults then had to deal with almost impenetrable barbed-wire entanglements erected in front of the trenches. The wire was always far enough away from the trenches that it stopped enemy soldiers at too great a distance for them to throw grenades into the trenches. One of the most dangerous jobs soldiers faced was having to leave their trenches at night to repair or extend the barbed wire entanglements. Even under pitch-black skies, they were likely to be shot at if they made any noise.

With rifles, machine guns, and mortars frequently fired between enemy trenches and grenades being tossed back and forth, the ground in no-man's-land areas was so badly devastated that plants ceased to grow there and the ground was pockmarked with holes and torn apart. When rains fell, the ground became so soft and sticky that soldiers would have found it difficult to cross even if they were not under fire, as they usually were. When the rains were especially heavy, pits filled with water. Many soldiers who got stuck in the muck actually drowned in puddles.

This photo, taken in northern France's Flanders Field shortly after the war, shows how devastated the terrain became in a typical no-man's-land.

Because removing wounded and dead soldiers from no-man's-land under enemy fire was extremely dangerous, dead soldiers and animals were often left where they fell until they rotted. Seeing one's comrades meet such grisly fates added to the miseries trench soldiers already had to endure. The stenches rising from nearby decomposing bodies made things even worse and added health hazards. After the war, an American army officer writing about the difficulty of keeping perishable foods such as meats and vegetables sanitary commented on "the immense amount of decay all along the front. All those rotten woods were filled with dead horses, dead men, the refuse, excrement and the garbage of armies. The ground must have been literally alive with pus and decay germs."

When armies prepared to launch major assaults on enemy positions, they routinely began with artillery barrages that could last for days and sometimes fire more than one million shells. A British soldier described what it was like to be the target of a major barrage:

A diabolical uproar surrounds us. We are conscious of a sustained crescendo, an incessant multiplication of the universal frenzy; a hurricane of hoarse and hollow banging of raging clamour, of piercing and beast-like screams, fastens furiously with

tatters of smoke upon the earth where we are buried up to our necks, and the wind of the shells seems to set it heaving and pitching.

Some soldiers cracked under the strain and experienced what was then known as "shell shock" and was later more commonly called "combat fatigue" or "post-traumatic stress disorder." An American private recalled how badly the barrages could affect men:

The nights were continuously disturbed… by the cries of shell-shocked men. Most of those outbursts began with a howling peal of laughter, a laugh to make one's skin creep and his hair rise, and ended in a shuddering wail, frequently followed by tears…. These men had became totally insane, and some of them caused no little trouble to their comrades trying to take care of them.

Surprisingly, however, long artillery barrages were often ineffective. Whenever a barrage occurred, it was a dead giveaway of where the enemy would next attack. Moreover, dugouts in the backline trenches at which the heaviest barrages were directed were often dug so deep that even prolonged barrages did little damage to them. Barrages could even

Cook Maconochie Stew

THE QUALITY AND quantity of food provided to trench soldiers varied among the different armies and at different times. During the first years of the war, most Allied soldiers ate adequately when supply lines were not disrupted and their trenches were not being bombarded. However, keeping millions of soldiers fed became more difficult as the home countries ran short on food and German submarine attacks on supply ships made transporting goods harder.

One of the most common meals eaten by British troops was Maconochie (*mack-oh-nack-ee*) stew, a precooked, canned dish manufactured by a Scottish company. It was regarded as tolerably edible when eaten hot but was hard to get down when it was cold. You can easily make a stew similar to wartime Maconochie and learn what a typical trench dinner tasted like.

Adult supervision required

Ingredients
- 12 ounces beef (or one can of corned beef)
- 5 ounces boiling potatoes
- 1 ounce onions
- 1 ounce carrots
- 1 ounce beans, cooked (white beans such as navy or great northern)
- Water
- 1 tablespoon fat (lard or rendered beef fat)
- ¼ cup beef stock or water
- 1 tablespoon flour
- Salt

Utensils
- Knife
- Potato peeler
- Cutting board
- 1-quart cooking pot
- Cooking pan
- Small mixing bowl
- Stirring spoon

If you use fresh beef, cut it into pieces no larger than 1 inch across. You can substitute a can of corned beef if necessary. Peel the potatoes and cut them and the onions and carrots into thin slices. Put all the meat and vegetables, including the beans, in a cooking pot and cover with enough water to steam or boil them until they are tender. Heat the fat in a pan and then add the cooked beef and vegetables. Mix the flour with beef stock or water in a small mixing bowl to make a batter and stir it into the stew. Add salt to taste and allow the stew to cool before eating it.

When you eat your stew, think of what it would be like to eat the same dish almost every day for several years. Keep in mind that your stew probably uses better ingredients than those in the original Maconochie stew.

MACONOCHIE'S

WORLD-FAMOUS RATIONS.

BEEF
POTATOES
HARICOTS
CARROTS
ONIONS
about
22 ozs
NETT.

HOT MACONOCHIE

A RICH, DELICIOUS STEW !

READY COOKED

1s. 6d. per tin.

A SUSTAINING AND ECONOMICAL MEAL FOR A FAMILY.

SAVES FUEL, TIME and LABOUR. ASK YOUR GROCER FOR IT.

Collection of the author

be counterproductive. Despite the improved accuracy of modern artillery weapons, many shells fell short of their targets, tearing up the ground through which the attacking forces had to advance to reach the enemy. Badly broken-up ground slowed down the advances, and if rain intervened, shell-pocked ground could be virtually impassable.

Another technique for assaulting enemy positions was to dig tunnels deep under no-man's-land in order to plant large explosive charges directly under enemy trenches. This kind of work, aptly known as mining, required the specialized skills of real miners. Consequently, both sides employed soldiers experienced in coal mining to do the tunneling and plant explosives. It was exceedingly dangerous work because of the hazards of collapsing tunnels and prematurely bursting explosives. Occasionally, miners digging their way toward enemy trenches ran directly into enemy soldiers digging in the opposite direction for the same reason. However, when mining schemes were successful, the results could be highly effective: One moment soldiers could be relaxing in their trenches with no expectation of unusual danger. The next moment they could be blown to bits. On one occasion, British miners put so much explosive material under a German trench near the French coast, its explosion was heard in England.

Daily Routines

SOLDIERS STATIONED at the front spent only a small part of their time in actual combat. In fact, it was not unusual for individual soldiers to spend several months on the western front without even seeing a single enemy soldier. This is not to say that they were necessarily safe when not fighting. They might not see an enemy while they were on the frontlines, but if they climbed out of their trenches, unseen enemies were likely to spot them, with lethal consequences. Even during generally quiet periods, enemy artillery shells occasionally dropped into trenches, killing and wounding soldiers. Even when shells killed no one, their explosions could demoralize troops. An American private described thinking "the whole world was coming to an end" when a shell exploded near him.

Because of the danger of moving outside the trenches in daylight, soldiers did much of their work at night under the protection of darkness. Daylight hours they typically spent resting and engaging in personal matters, such as cleaning and repairing their clothes and equipment and writing letters home.

The German, British, French, and, later, American armies all had different routines. All these armies regularly rotated units through their front, supply, and reserve lines and among

Press a Flower to Send Home from the Front

ONE WAY TRENCH soldiers passed idle time was by picking wild flowers, pressing them, and mailing them home to loved ones as mementos of the front. While future US president Harry S. Truman was serving in the US Army in France, he occasionally sent pressed flowers to his cousin and his fiancée. He did not want to advertise that fact for fear of being teased by fellow soldiers, but he was not the only soldier sending flowers home.

Flower pressing is a 500-year-old technique that can attain high levels of artistic expression. Artists work with special flower presses, but soldiers in the field had no special equipment. You can do what they did to press flowers for a school project, for note cards or greeting cards, or for your own enjoyment.

Materials

- ✪ Fresh flowers
- ✪ Scissors
- ✪ Cotton balls or tissues
- ✪ Colorless blotting paper or other absorbent paper
- ✪ A heavy book, such as a big phone book
- ✪ White glue
- ✪ Art paper, card stock, or note cards

Begin by picking several fresh flowers whose petals lend themselves well to attractive flattening, such as lilacs, daisies, and poppies. Experiment with a variety of colors and types of flowers. The best time to collect them is in the morning, after dew has evaporated from their petals and leaves. Use scissors to cut the stems close to the petals.

Next, remove residual moisture by dabbing the flowers gently with cotton balls or tissues. After the flowers are as dry as possible, lay each one flat on at least one piece of smooth, absorbent, and colorless paper. (Avoid patterned paper towels that may make visible impressions on the flowers.)

Lay a large, heavy book on a flat surface and open it to its last pages. Place one of the flowers on a page, with absorbent paper above and below it. If you need to protect the book, place additional layers of paper between the absorbent sheets and the book's pages. (Do not use someone else's book without permission!) If you are pressing more than one flower at a time, allow at least 1/8 inch of pages between the flowers.

Proper drying can take two to three weeks, depending on the climate and how much moisture is in the flowers. It does not hurt to check the flowers occasionally, however, and you can speed up their drying by replacing the absorbent paper if it feels damp.

When the flowers are completely dry, you can use white glue to attach them to letters, note cards, or posters or to make elaborate designs. The ideal flower for a World War I project would be a red poppy, which became a postwar symbol of remembrance.

Red Poppy from Verdun Found growing in the shadow of Fort Douaumont by Captain Harry S. Truman, Battery D, 129th Field Artillery October 1918.

A poppy Harry S. Truman found in the rubble of Verdun and sent to his cousin.

Harry S. Truman Presidential Library and Museum

different sectors. When soldiers changed their posts, they had to carry all their personal equipment with them. Each British soldier's sleeping gear, clothes, weapons, drinking water, eating utensils, shovels, other equipment, and personal items typically weighed from 60 to 80 pounds—all of which he carried on his back on grueling marches as long as 10 to 20 miles. French and German soldiers typically carried even heavier equipment.

One British soldier estimated that in 1916 alone he had to relocate 80 times—mostly on foot, sometimes on trains. Frequent moves taxed soldiers' strength but had the compensating virtue of helping to relieve boredom. German regiments tended to stay at the same posts for much longer periods.

A typical day for a trench soldier started early in the morning with an hour-long "stand to," in which every soldier mounted the fire step in his trench to be ready for an enemy attack. The rest of the day was divided into watch cycles in which soldiers rotated sentry duties to maintain a constant watch for enemy activity. Meanwhile, other soldiers did such work as repairing the trenches, cleaning their rifles and gear, fetching food and supplies from support trenches, and tending to the wounded. The trenches themselves were usually in constant need of work, especially when intruding water was a problem. Excess water had to be removed, trench walls had to be strengthened, new trench lines and latrines had to be dug, and so on.

When soldiers were not on watch or engaged in work details, they played card games, wrote letters home, or read books. Some soldiers kept pets such as dogs and cats or wild animals they captured and tamed.

Special Discomforts

THE COMBINATION of dull day-to-day routines and the constant danger of being killed or wounded made the lives of trench soldiers unpleasant. However, the special conditions that the trenches themselves created made the soldiers' lives even more miserable.

To combat the cold in winter months, soldiers burned wood chips and coke (coal residue) on small metal containers within their crowded dugouts. Frozen shoes could be a problem. One American soldier recalled how "at night, the boys would take off their shoes and leave them near their bunks, the shoes would freeze, and on several mornings when they could not get them on they were compelled to put a piece of paper in the shoes and set it on fire to melt the ice. They could then pour out the water and put them on."

Unventilated smoke combined with wretched smells and dankness to make for a very

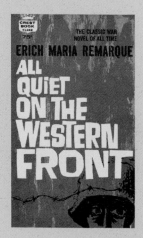

ALL QUIET ON THE WESTERN FRONT

The most famous novel to come out of World War I was written by the German war veteran Erich Marie Remarque and was published in English in 1929 as *All Quiet on the Western Front*. Praised for its realistic depiction of the grim conditions in trench warfare, it follows the experiences of a young German soldier named Paul Bäumer. He and many of his schoolmates enlist in the army after being stirred by their schoolmaster's promise that heroic action and glory await them. What the young soldiers experience, however, is not glory but dreary boredom and suffering punctuated by inglorious deaths. The best of several screen adaptations is the film made in 1930, when memories of the horror of the war were still fresh.

unpleasant atmosphere. A marine sergeant recalled that the French dugout in which he was stationed "didn't have ventilating systems on account of the gas danger. I have never experienced such foul air as when I slept in dugouts when I was with the French." To make matters worse, the absence of chimneys occasionally caused soldiers to suffocate in their sleep as the fires burned up oxygen. Poison gases, which are discussed in a later chapter, were especially hazardous to soldiers in trenches. Heavier than air, they flowed down to the ground and collected in trenches.

One of the worst aspects of trenches, however, was their filthiness. Maintaining sanitary conditions was often impossible. Frontline soldiers could not bathe regularly, trash was difficult to remove, soldiers did not always use the latrine pits to relieve themselves, and sometimes the dead bodies of men and animals could not be fully removed. In fact, as the war wore on, new trenches were often dug into places where dead soldiers and animals had been buried earlier.

Dead bodies and discarded food scraps attracted large numbers of rats, which multiplied rapidly. Rats overran most frontline trenches. Nearly impossible to exterminate, the loathsome creatures boldly raided food supplies, which they contaminated while also spreading diseases. A British soldier writing home from the front described the place where he was stationed as being overrun by "thousands" of rats:

You cannot put a mouthful down but what they won't pinch it. We have to suspend our food in sandbags from the roofs of our dugouts, and wake up in the night, to find them having a swing on the bags, cheeky rascals. We have to cover our faces at night as several men have been bitten, and we only have our greatcoats for cover, we keep our boots and putties [leggings] on to protect our legs. They crawl over you at night...

Colonel Frederick M. Wise of the US Marine Corps, who served in the trenches in 1917, marveled over the size of the rats he saw and described his unusual encounter with one:

I was walking down the trench one day when a rat on one side saw me come along. He waited until I got opposite him, leaped to my shoulder, and before I could knock him off, leaped to the other side of the trench. He had used me deliberately as a stepping-stone to save him the trouble of climbing down to the bottom of that trench and climbing out the other side.

The second major type of vermin that infested trenches were lice. These tiny parasites multiplied on soldiers' bodies and in their clothes. Biting the skin of their hosts, the lice caused painful itching and carried a disease known as trench fever. By themselves, lice accounted for a large percentage of sick cases that took soldiers out of action. During the warm summer months, trenches were filled with flies, which swarmed over exposed food and the soldiers themselves. An American artilleryman wrote a vivid description of them:

Flies—millions and millions of them. In spots, the air is black with the cloud of them. At mess you get a dish full of stuff, carry it away to a shady spot and sit down to eat. When you get there it is covered with flies so thick, that an observer would think we had "currant pudding," for every meal thruout the day.... If you are lucky, you don't swallow one or more insects. If you are not—then the fly is unlucky too.

Other insect pests contributing to the soldiers' misery included nits, itch mites, and fleas. Chemicals used to fight these vermin added to the already sickening stenches prevailing in the trenches.

Frontline trench conditions were often horrifying, but most individual soldiers did not have to endure them for long stretches. Policies varied among the different armies on the western front, but most soldiers spent less than a week at any one time in the frontlines before being rotated out. The rest of the time they spent in safer and cleaner support and reserve trenches, at bases away from the front, and on leave. Nevertheless, by the end of the war, more soldiers succumbed to sickness and disease caused by trench conditions than suffered battle casualties.

Despite the miseries soldiers endured, life in the trenches was not always bad. One British soldier wrote home to tell about the

good times in the trenches, especially in the summer. Plenty of grub, ripping weather, a decent dugout for two, and sentry duty for only one hour in seventeen. We loafed about visiting our friends in other dugouts, reading or writing our letters with nothing to worry us, and when the afternoon sun became too hot we got into the shady dugout and lay there watching the moles and lizards crawling about the empty trench. Yes, that was a fine spell.

4
OTHER FRONTS

WORLD WAR I was dubbed a world war because it was fought over a large part of the globe. The outcome of the war was decided mostly by events in Europe, especially on the western front, but fighting in other parts of the world also had important consequences. To many observers, the European fronts were the "main events" and other fronts were merely "sideshows," but those other fronts were equally dangerous to the people involved in them.

After western Europe, the second most important war zone was eastern Europe, where the war had originally started. Major battles were also fought in the Middle East and in four parts of Africa, and significant naval battles were fought far from all these places. Most surprisingly, perhaps, the last battles of the war were fought in East Africa, where the war may be said to have finally ended.

The Eastern Front

As the first chapter shows, the war grew out of a regional conflict in southeastern Europe's Balkan peninsula. Serbian nationalists there had sought to separate Bosnia-Herzegovina from the Austro-Hungarian Empire and join it to a greater Slavic state. When Austria-Hungary declared war on Serbia, Russia rallied to its fellow Slavs' defense by mobilizing its army, while Germany mobilized to back its ally, Austria-Hungary. Serbia would take a heavy beating in the conflict that followed, and other countries in the region would be drawn into the war, but the main fight pitted Russia against Germany and Austria-Hungary.

Germany had little interest in Balkan affairs. Its real reason for getting involved in that conflict was to take on Russia and reduce its power before it could modernize its huge army and become a threat to Germany itself. Germany's prewar Schlieffen Plan called for it to knock France out of the war in the west rapidly so it could move its victorious troops east to take on Russia. The plan was based on the assumption that Russia would be so slow to mobilize, Germany could defeat it before its military was at full strength.

Two things prevented the Schlieffen Plan from working. First, France could not be knocked out quickly as anticipated, forcing Germany to leave most of its troops on the western front. Second, Russia mobilized faster than expected and quickly challenged Germany and Austria-Hungary from the east. Germany thus found itself in exactly the situation it had hoped to avoid: fighting a two-front war against strong enemies.

In 1914, Russia was by far the largest country in Europe in both population and area—most of which was actually in Asia. Thanks to its great size it also had the largest army. However, the strength of its army was handicapped by a lack of modern weapons and equipment, inadequate training, and poor leadership, especially in the top levels of government. Tsar Nicholas II was a weak emperor whose indecisiveness and sometimes foolish decisions would seriously damage Russia's war efforts. Unpopular within his own country and facing many internal crises, he had a fragile hold on his government. His best bet would have been to stay out of the war, but he apparently hoped a military victory would strengthen his government. As events would show, neither he nor his government would survive the war.

On August 4, 1914, three days after it had declared war on Russia and its western foes, Germany sent troops into Poland, which was then part of the Russian Empire. Two weeks later, Russia countered by invading both Austria-Hungary and Germany's East Prus-

THE EASTERN FRONT

Make a World War I Scoreboard

WORLD WAR I was so big and complicated that it is difficult to keep track of all the countries involved in it. To make doing that easier, you can construct a large "scoreboard" in the form of a table that lists the most important facts about each country. Such a table might look something like the one below:

Materials

✪ Sheet of construction paper or poster board at least 24 inches wide and 36 inches long
✪ Ruler or other drafting tool for drawing straight lines

✪ Pencil and pen
✪ Access to additional reference materials about the war

Using a pencil and ruler or other drafting tool suitable for making straight lines, draw a table with at least seven columns and 37 rows. You can use the incomplete table below as a model to estimate how much space each cell in your table will need. If you wish to include more information than the sample table has, add more columns. After outlining your table with a pencil, use an ink pen to darken its final lines and to fill in its text.

Fill in the names of nations directly involved in the war in the first column in approximate order of their entry into to the war, and then start filling in the other columns. You will need to find information on countries discussed in this book in other sources. For additional information, consult some of the books or websites listed in the Resources section at the back of this book.

After completing the table as fully as you can, you will have a summary of the war that can be mounted on a wall. An outline map of the world with the participant nations colored in would make a nice illustration to accompany the table.

PARTICIPANTS		ENTERED THE WAR				OUTCOME
Country	Region	Date	Reason	Side	Fate	Postwar Condition
Austria-Hungary	Europe	7/28/1914	To control the Balkans	Central Powers	Loss	Ended monarchy and dissolved empire
Serbia	Europe	7/28/1914	To resist Austro-Hungarian invasion	Allied Powers		Absorbed into new nation later known as Yugoslavia
Russia	Europe	8/1/1914	To support Serbia	Allied Powers	Exited	Ended monarchy, endured civil war, and had communist revolution
Germany	Europe	8/1/1914	To support Austria-Hungary	Central Powers	Loss	Replaced monarchy with democratic government and saddled with heavy reparations
France	Europe	8/3/1914	To resist German invasion	Allied Powers	Win	Regained lost French lands and gained Middle Eastern territories
Belgium	Europe	8/3/1914	To resist Germany	Allied Powers	Win	Independence restored
Luxembourg	Europe	8/3/1914	Conquered by Germany	—		Independence restored
Great Britain	Europe	8/4/1914	To defend Belgium	Allied Powers	Win	Gained Middle Eastern territories
Japan	Asia	8/23/1914	To win German colonies in the Pacific	Allied Powers		
South Africa	Africa		To capture German Southwest Africa	Allied Powers		

sia region bordering Poland. The first Russian army into Austria-Hungary pushed well into the country, whose invasion of Serbia was also going badly. Austria-Hungary would not be able to subdue Serbia until it got German and Bulgarian help.

Meanwhile, the Russian armies entering Germany caught the Germans by surprise, showing that Russia was mobilizing much faster than had been expected. When that Russian advance threatened the German regional capital, Königsberg (now Kaliningrad, Russia), the local commander nervously wanted to call a retreat. However, the German high command replaced him with the more experienced general Paul von Hindenburg and sent troops from the western front to help in East Prussia.

Russia's early advantage was soon lost because of lack of coordination between its two principal army commanders, Generals Alexander Samsonov and Paul von Rennenkampf, who detested each other. Their refusal to support each other allowed Hindenburg's reinforced army to defeat them one at a time. On August 26, the Germans destroyed Samsonov's army in the Battle of Tannenberg. Samsonov himself committed suicide later the same day.

With Samsonov's army out of the way, the Germans routed Rennenkampf's army in the Battle of the Masurian Lakes on September 9. Rennenkampf successfully retreated with what

General Paul von Hindenburg (left) and his chief of staff on the eastern front, Erich von Ludendorff.

remained of his army, but by then the two Russian armies had lost about 300,000 soldiers in only a few weeks of fighting. Even gigantic Russia could not afford to lose troops at that rate.

Germany had prevailed in its first head-on encounters with Russia, but having to withdraw troops from the western front derailed its grand Schlieffen Plan. Whatever else Europe's warring nations learned during the first month of fighting, it was becoming evident that the war would last longer in both the west and the east than anyone had predicted.

East Asia

WHILE HEAVY fighting was going on in western and eastern Europe, Japan became the first Asian nation to enter the conflict when it declared war on Germany on August 23. Almost a decade earlier, it had decisively defeated Russia in the Russo-Japanese War. By 1914, it had a modern army and navy rivaling those of Europe's major powers. It had signed a treaty of alliance with Great Britain in 1902 but was not interested in being drawn into the European land war. Its primary interest was seizing control of the German colonies scattered between the coast of China and the South Pacific. Japan's motives in the war may have been self-serving, but by taking access to secure bases and refueling stations away from German naval

squadrons operating in the Pacific, Japan made the Pacific and Indian Oceans safer for Allied shipping and helped drive German warships to their doom off South America.

Turkey and the Dardanelles

THE FOURTH great empire to enter the war was the old Turkish Ottoman Empire, whose rule had once extended over Turkey, the Balkans, parts of eastern Europe, North Africa, and much of the eastern Mediterranean region. By the early 20th century, however, revolts, foreign wars, and government mismanagement had reduced the empire to its Turkish core, parts of the Balkan Peninsula, and most of the Middle East region from Asia Minor in the north to what is now Saudi Arabia in the south.

Decaying from long years of poverty and inefficient and corrupt government at all levels, the Ottoman Empire was often disparaged as the "sick man of Europe." As an ally, the empire promised to be more a drain on manpower and resources than a contributor to the war effort for either side. However, Turkey had one great asset that both the Allies and Central

Trenches used on the eastern front did not approach western front trenches in size and complexity. Here Russian soldiers await a German attack in a temporary trench.

National Geographic Magazine (1917, vol. 31, p. 379)

Powers coveted: control over the Dardanelles Strait that separated European Turkey from its Asia Minor provinces. It was the channel connecting the Mediterranean and Black Seas.

The Black Sea to Turkey's north was the back door to Russia and eastern Europe. The Dardanelles was the key to that door. Through it, ships could carry weapons, troops, and goods to supply Russia or to support an invasion of the Central Powers from their rear. Consequently, both the Allies and the Central Powers courted Turkish friendship as the war was beginning. Germany's Kaiser Wilhelm II felt a special empathy toward the Middle East's Islamic religion after visiting Turkey in 1889 and was keen to win Turkey's friendship.

Turkish machine gunners fighting under German officers at the Dardanelles.

Ultimately, diplomatic blunders on Britain's part moved Turkey's government to lean toward the Germans. In October 1914, an unusual incident in the Mediterranean led to Germany winning a Turkish alliance. After a British naval squadron chased two German warships across the Mediterranean, the German ships took refuge in the harbor of Turkey's capital, Constantinople (now Istanbul). Knowing that Britain's Royal Navy would never allow the ships to re-enter the Mediterranean, the German government turned them over to Turkey. The Turks were especially gratified to acquire the modern warships because the British government had recently commandeered two brand-new battleships built in Scotland for Turkey and for which the Turks had already paid.

Although Turkey technically bought the two German ships, which now flew under Turkish flags, the ships were still manned by German officers and crew and were still taking their orders from Germany. In late October, the ships bombarded Russian towns on the Black Sea, effectively declaring war against Russia in the name of Turkey. In early November, Russia and Serbia declared war on Turkey, and Britain and France soon followed with declarations of their own.

At that time future British prime minister Winston S. Churchill was the first lord of the British Admiralty. In that office, he pushed hard for an Allied invasion of Turkey with the object of taking control of the Dardanelles so the Allies could connect Russian ports with the Mediterranean and make possible an assault on the Central Powers from the Black Sea. To capture the Dardanelles, the Allies needed to occupy Turkey's Gallipoli Peninsula on the west side of the narrow strait.

Churchill encountered strong opposition within the British government to his invasion plan because it would require diverting desperately needed troops from the western front to the eastern Mediterranean. Eventually, however, he prevailed by proposing the entire invasion be undertaken by the British and French navies. The plan called for a fleet of battleships to sail up the Aegean Sea, enter the Dardanelles Strait, and use their big guns to bombard Turkish coastal forts as they pushed north. The joint naval attack began in mid-March 1915 but quickly collapsed. Five of the fleet's 16 battleships were almost immediately sunk or disabled by Turkish mines in the water. The Allied commanders withdrew their fleet.

Afterward, a new Allied plan was drawn up. It called for landing ground forces on the western coast of Gallipoli to capture the Turkish forts. The new assault began on April 25. This time the Allied force included large contingents of Australian and New Zealand ground troops from the opposite side of the globe. Its

initial landing was almost uncontested. However, after the Turks began pouring in large numbers of fresh troops, the situation became another stalemated war zone.

As on the western front, both sides fought hard and bravely, with neither gaining a significant advantage. By the time the Allies finally withdrew the following January, both sides had

Armenian refugee camp. A great human tragedy connected to the war was Turkish oppression of Christian Armenians in the Ottoman Empire. When Turkey tried to deport about 1.75 million Armenians to Syria and Mesopotamia, about 600,000 of them were murdered or died from exposure and starvation.

lost hundreds of thousands of men. The losses were felt especially hard in Australia and New Zealand. The Dardanelles would remain in Turkish hands for the rest of the war. The failed Allied campaign brought down British prime minister Herbert Henry Asquith's government and cost Churchill his position in the Admiralty. His career was far from over, however. The editor of the London *Observer* pointed out that Churchill was still young and had "lion-hearted courage. No number of enemies can fight down his ability and force. His hour of triumph will come." During the second world war, Churchill would lead Great Britain to victory.

While the Gallipoli campaign was going on, other nations in that region entered the war. Bulgaria, which bordered the Black Sea and separated Serbia and Turkey, joined the Central Powers in an invasion of Serbia in October 1915. Its chief goal was to take control of Macedonia to its south to gain direct access to the Aegean Sea. Romania, to Bulgaria's north, would join the Allies in August 1916, putting that neighbor at war against Bulgaria, Austria-Hungary, and Germany.

Greece, to Turkey's south, maintained an uneasy neutrality through the first year of the war. The country had long distrusted Turkey but hesitated to align itself with the Allies, which pressed it to join them. Rivalries within the Greek government complicated matters.

Greece finally declared war on the Central Powers in June 1917.

Mesopotamia

TURKEY'S ENTRY into the war on the side of the Central Powers opened its Middle Eastern territories to possible Allied invasion. Most of those territories were impoverished, underdeveloped, and of little interest to the European powers. However, some of them had rich oil fields that were increasing in strategic importance as petroleum-driven vehicles were gaining importance throughout the world. Petroleum was particularly valuable for warships, which were turning to fuel oil instead of coal. An Allied invasion of Mesopotamia was not long in coming.

On November 5, 1914, a joint British and British Indian force occupied the Ottoman port of Basra at the northern end of the Persian Gulf in what is now southern Iraq. There the Allies took control of the oil fields. Over the ensuing months, British forces pushed farther inland. Eventually, however, the Turks turned the tables on the invaders and captured virtually the entire British invasion force in April 1916.

Farther south, the Allies encouraged Arab nationalists to revolt against Ottoman rule in order to divert Turkish troops and resources from other war zones. This was the region in which the British officer and Arab scholar T. E. Lawrence gained fame as "Lawrence of Arabia." He rallied Arabs and personally led attacks on Turkish posts and troop trains. He began working with Arab leaders in October 1916 in what later became Saudi Arabia. Over the next two years he helped lead successful campaigns against the Turks in Palestine and Syria.

As a dedicated advocate of Arab nationalism, he strongly supported Arab independence—a goal that would conflict with Britain's postwar aims in the Middle East.

The Turks wanted to hold on to their Middle Eastern territories, but they also had other aims. One of their chief goals was to capture Egypt's Suez Canal. That artificial waterway

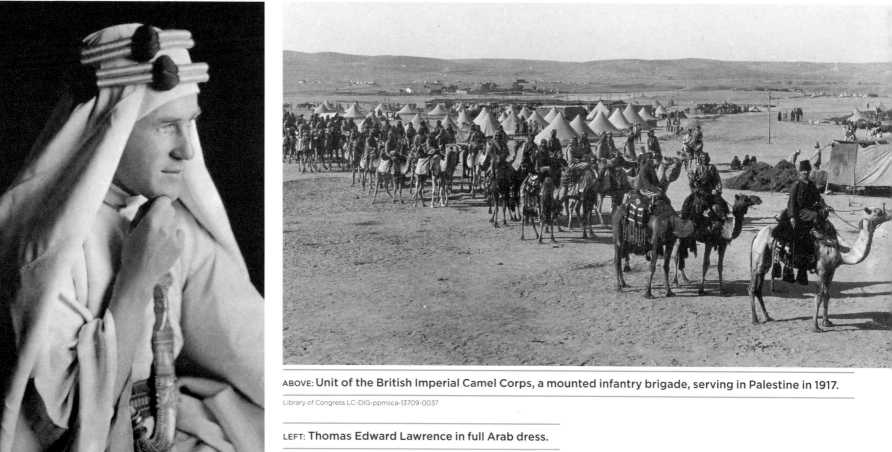

ABOVE: **Unit of the British Imperial Camel Corps, a mounted infantry brigade, serving in Palestine in 1917.**

Library of Congress LC-DIG-ppmsca-13709-0037

LEFT: **Thomas Edward Lawrence in full Arab dress.**

Lowell Thomas, *With Lawrence in Arabia* (1919)

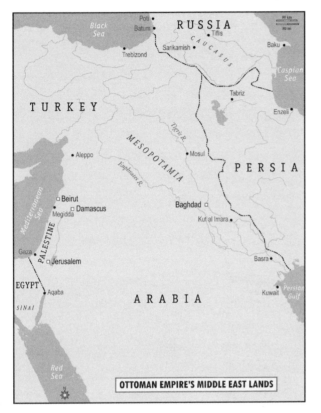

OTTOMAN EMPIRE'S MIDDLE EAST LANDS

connected the Mediterranean Sea with the Red Sea and the Indian Ocean. It was a vital route for moving troops and supplies from British India to Europe. However, the British kept enough troops in Egypt to protect the canal throughout the war.

Africa

DURING THE late 19th century, Germany had been one of the leaders in the European scramble to grab colonies in Africa. The big winners in that race were Britain and France, which together had seized control of most of sub-Saharan Africa by 1914. Germany had accumulated four widely separated colonies (technically known as "protectorates"). The smallest was Togoland (now Togo), a narrow sliver of territory on West Africa's Guinea Coast. The next largest was Kamerun (now Cameroon), an equatorial territory east of Nigeria on the Gulf of Guinea. German Southwest Africa (now Namibia), Germany's largest colony, bordered the Union of South Africa on the south Atlantic coast. Germany's richest colony, however, was German East Africa (later split into Tanganyika and Ruanda-Urundi; now divided among Rwanda, Burundi, and Tanzania), just south of the equator on the Indian Ocean coast.

Surrounded by colonies of Allied Powers, including Portugal, none of the German col-

onies was easily defensible, and only Southwest Africa had a substantial defense force. Germany had acquired the colonies to serve as sources of raw products for German industry and consumption. It had also planted substantial numbers of German settlers in its southwest and east colonies. Because Britain's Royal Navy virtually commanded the world's oceans, the war cut Germany off from its colonies so that it could neither benefit from their products nor provide support against Allied invasions. Surrounded by hostile neighbors, each German colony was on its own. Allied forces moved against the German colonies almost immediately after the war began. Their main strategic objective was to seize control of ports and radio facilities that could be used to aid German warships still at sea.

Togoland had a minuscule German population and was defended only by a small paramilitary police force manned by African recruits. In early August 1914, British and French troops from neighboring colonies advanced into the territory, which surrendered a few weeks later.

Although Kamerun was only average in size by African standards, it was larger than both France and Germany combined. Nevertheless, it was defended by only 200 German and 1,500 African troops, along with more than 1,000 mostly African paramilitary police. The sheer size of the colony combined with its unhealthy climate and difficult terrain to make its conquest a far more difficult challenge than that posed by Togoland. The British and French campaign against Kamerun lasted from late September 1914 into January 1916. It eventually involved more than 18,000 Allied troops, including Africans from other colonies, and killed more than 4,000 of them. The Germans suffered an unknown number of casualties.

The Allied conquest of German Southwest Africa was a very different and more difficult affair. In contrast to Germany's other African colonies, Southwest Africa had about 15,000 German settlers and an arid, open terrain that made rapid troop movements over immense areas possible. Its defense force with 3,000 professional German troops presented a formidable challenge to an invasion force. Southwest's southern neighbor, the Union of South Africa, had a far larger European settler population and much more substantial military force of its own that included many battle-hardened veterans of the recent South African (Boer) War.

After the war began, South African prime minister Louis Botha immediately offered to send South African military forces to aid Britain in the European war. Britain's immediate response was to ask South Africa to use its military to seize German Southwest Africa. It was an attractive offer to South Africa's lead-

ers, who saw in it the possibility of annexing German Southwest Africa to their own country.

The South African campaign against Southwest began in September. With the help of Britain's Royal Navy, one South African force landed at a port on the west, while a second force entered the colony overland from the east. Meanwhile, troops from British Southern Rhodesia to the north occupied Southwest's Caprivi Strip, the colony's northeastern

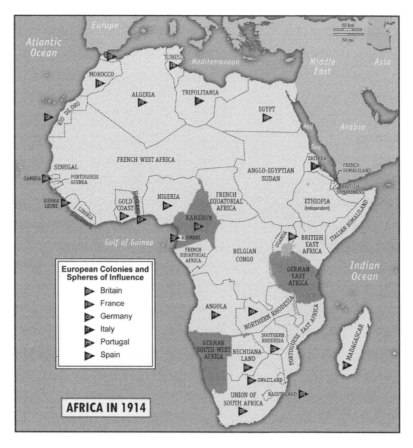

panhandle. In the wide open spaces of the colony, the ensuing conflict had similarities to the Allies' World War II campaign against German forces in North Africa. Much of the effort in the campaign went into simply pursuing the German units from place to place.

South Africa's campaign in Southwest Africa might have ended quickly, were it not for a revolt against the South African government that broke out in October. Afrikaners (Boers), still bitter about their defeat in the South African War, resented British influence in their country, even though its government was led by Botha and other fellow Afrikaners. Sympathetic toward Germany, the approximately 11,000 men participating in the so-called Boer Rebellion wanted South Africa to leave German Southwest alone and to make South Africa fully independent of Britain. Their revolt lasted well into 1915, delaying the Southwest Africa campaign and giving Germans there more time to prepare their defenses.

In February 1915, after South African general Jan Christiaan Smuts had led the suppression of the rebellion, he resumed South Africa's campaign in Southwest. The German governor finally surrendered in July. Almost 150,000 troops in South African units would eventually fight for the Allies in Europe and other parts of Africa before the war was over. Another 10,000 served in other Allied forces.

Only men of European descent were allowed to serve in South African combat units, but about 85,000 nonwhite South African volunteers served in labor battalions and other support services in Europe.

German East Africa's resistance to Allied conquest is one of the most remarkable stories of the entire war. Under the leadership of General Paul Emil von Lettow-Vorbeck, the German forces in that colony evaded capture for more than four years and did not surrender until two weeks after the war had ended in Europe. Although his troops were cut off from outside German support, Lettow-Vorbeck kept them moving almost continuously throughout the war, harassing enemy posts and railroads across the borders and disrupting parts of German East that were occupied by the British.

Lettow-Vorbeck began his defensive campaign with only 260 European troops and about 2,500 well-trained African troops, who were known as *askaris* in the Swahili language. His contingent also contained more than 2,000 mostly African police and several thousand African bearers who carried supplies and equipment. Over the course of his campaign, he managed to increase those numbers. By maintaining strict discipline and personally sharing in the severe discomforts his troops suffered in East Africa's harsh tropical conditions, Lettow-Vorbeck not only kept his forces together, but he also kept them so dangerous that the Allies could not simply ignore them. He constantly improvised to maintain supplies and employed innovative guerrilla tactics to evade capture. Through four years of fighting, he marched his men through the interior of German East and even raided in Portuguese East Africa (now Mozambique) and Northern Rhodesia (now Zambia), where he finally surrendered in November 1918.

In the context of World War I as a whole, German East Africa was inconsequential. However, Lettow-Vorbeck's campaign forced Britain to send in tens of thousands of troops and supplies that could have been used more profitably elsewhere. In January 1916, the South African general Jan Christiaan Smuts took overall command of the Allied invasion in German East and brought more than 30,000 South African troops with him. He succeeded in taking control of most of the colony, but despite his considerable experience in fighting in Southern Africa, even he could not run down Lettow-Vorbeck in a full year of campaigning.

Contemporary German card honoring General Lettow-Vorbeck, German East Africa governor Heinrich Schnee, and African askaris.

5

THE WEAPONS OF WAR

ONE OF THE most important things to understand about World War I is the momentous changes new technologies brought to warfare. Almost every major conflict of the past several centuries has been influenced by at least one new invention or other technology not available in earlier wars. Obvious examples range from more powerful and easier-to-use firearms, steam-powered warships, and telegraphic communications during the 19th century to the GPS guidance tools, "smart bombs," and drone reconnaissance aircraft of our modern age.

What sets World War I apart from other wars is both the large number of technological innovations used and the enormity of their impact on the conduct of the war itself. The war's new weapons, forms of transportation, and forms of communication greatly

changed the ways in which all future wars would be fought. That is important in itself, but another aspect of these changes should be considered—how they affected the ways in which military decisions were made. In general, it is fair to say that military and government leaders on both sides of the war did not always know how the new technologies should be used and were often surprised by their impacts.

This chapter examines broad categories of technologies whose innovations were especially important in World War I. Emphasis is placed on innovations affecting land fighting. Innovations in naval and aviation technology are covered in later chapters.

Machine Guns

IN ITS broadest sense, a "machine gun" is a weapon that can fire numerous rounds of ammunition rapidly and continuously. The earliest machine guns were the American-made Gatling guns first used in the US Civil War during the 1860s. Gatlings fired bullets through six or more separate barrels wrapped around a drum mounted on a carriage rotated by a hand crank as bullets fell into the barrels automatically. Gatling guns could fire as many as 200 rounds per minute but were cumbersome to move and operate and were not terribly accurate.

In its modern sense, a machine gun does what Gatling guns did but fires itself automatically. The first true machine gun was made by another American inventor, Hiram Maxim, in 1884. The Maxim gun used the recoil energy of each round to eject the spent cartridge, load the next round, cock its own bolt, strike the round to fire a bullet, and then repeat the process. All the operator had to do was aim the gun and squeeze its trigger for as long as he wished to fire. Maxim guns could fire much faster and more accurately than Gatlings. They were also more portable and easier to conceal from enemy return fire. These advantages made the Maxim a huge advance in lethal weaponry.

World War I machine guns were portable, but they nevertheless required three-to-six-man crews to operate and move them. Weighing 100 to 150 pounds each, they were usually mounted on heavy flat tripods. They could fire at speeds of 400 to 600 rounds per minute, using bullets fed into them on long cloth belts or shorter metal strips. Men operating the guns were kept busy feeding their ammunition, cooling their overheated barrels with water, and unjamming them when necessary. The guns were usually positioned close to one another in groups of three or four guns. A single gun had the firepower equivalent of as many as 60 to 80 rifles, so it should be clear why machine guns

Three-Minute Egg Camouflage Challenge

CAMOUFLAGE IS THE art of disguising objects to make them more difficult to see. If you duck behind a tree to keep from being seen, you are simply hiding. That is not camouflage. However, if you wear clothes and makeup that help you blend in with your surroundings, you are camouflaging yourself. In military combat, camouflage helps people avoid being shot by making them harder for enemies to see. Surprisingly, it was little used in warfare before the 20th century. In fact, many 19th-century armies outfitted soldiers in bright, colored uniforms that actually made them easier to see. When World War I started, French troops were still wearing blue jackets and bright red pants. However, the war's more advanced weapons made camouflaging more important than ever before, and troops in all armies were soon wearing uniforms with drab colors that were harder to see on battlefields. Aerial reconnaissance made it necessary to camouflage almost everything that could be an enemy target—people, guns, trucks, trains, airplanes, ships, supply dumps, buildings, and even roads.

This simple activity uses eggs to show how camouflaged objects are harder to spot than the same kinds of objects with bright colors.

Adult supervision required

Materials

- ✪ 1 dozen eggs
- ✪ Saucepan with cover
- ✪ Water
- ✪ Watercolor paints
- ✪ Paint brush
- ✪ Friend to serve as an assistant
- ✪ Stopwatch or other timing device
- ✪ Basket or sack in which to carry the eggs

To hard boil the eggs, place them in a saucepan and add enough cold water to cover them to a depth of at least one extra inch. With parental assistance, put the pan on a stove and bring the water to a full boil. After the water begins to boil hard, turn off the heat, cover the pan, and let it stand for about 12 minutes. Drain the warm water and refill the pan with cold water. After the eggs have cooled, pour out the water to let them dry.

Paint the upper halves of six eggs bright blue and their bottom halves bright red. For the remaining eggs, mix colors to create drab shades of green, brown, and yellow similar to those seen in a garden. Use these new colors to paint each egg with patterns resembling natural objects such as rocks and leaves. Your painting does not need to be neat, but it should cover all white surfaces.

While your friend is not looking, place each of the 12 eggs in a garden by itself. Do not hide the eggs but try to make them hard to spot—next to plants, in tall grass, and among branches and rocks. Give your friend a basket or sack in which to hold the eggs and allow the friend exactly three minutes to find as many of them as possible. When the time is up, count how many of each kind have been found. Then, repeat the challenge by having your friend redistribute all the eggs and time how long it takes you to find them.

The development of aircraft and observation balloons made it necessary to disguise objects on the ground from aerial reconnaissance. Here, artists train in methods of camouflaging installations on a model of a rural landscape.

Liberty's Victorious Conflict: A Photographic History of the World War (Chicago: Magazine Circulation Co., 1918)

Allied soldiers with a captured German machine gun.

enable small numbers of defenders to hold off more numerous enemies.

The first major conflict in which modern machine guns were extensively used was the Russo-Japanese War of 1904–1905. In fact, some historians regard that conflict, not World War I, as the first truly modern war. That war amply demonstrated how a handful of defenders could hold off assaults of much larger numbers of enemies with their machine guns. The Russo-Japanese War is also of special interest because it was closely watched by large numbers of military observers from other nations sent by their governments to study how new weapons were being used. These observers included army officers from Australia, Austria-Hungary, France, Germany, Great Britain, and the United States—all nations that later fought in World War I.

One lesson from the Russo-Japanese War the observers should have taken home was that machine guns gave such a powerful advantage to defensive positions that old combat strategies emphasizing offense would no longer work. Unfortunately, that lesson was not learned. As earlier chapters have shown, when armies tried to advance on the offensive during the early years of World War I, their regiments were simply shot to pieces by enemy machine guns. Both sides made the same mistakes. They responded by digging trenches to get soldiers out of the line of fire of machine guns.

Because of their size, comparatively cumbersome operating needs, and limited range compared to rifles, machine guns had limited uses as offensive weapons early in the war. As the war raged on, however, more lightweight models were developed. One of their most important applications was on airplanes, which by 1915 became strong enough to handle the extra weight of weapons. Machine guns were also used on naval vessels. Mounted on the decks of submarines, they were very valuable weapons when the subs surfaced to capture or sink enemy vessels.

The rifles individual soldiers used at the start of the war did not represent major technological advances over earlier models. They were, however, generally more accurate than earlier rifles and could be loaded and fired more rapidly. As the war progressed, rifles capable of automatically firing multiple rounds started appearing in combat. Rifles were effective as both offensive and defensive weapons, so improvements in their design gave neither offense nor defense a new advantage over the other. They did, however, increase the efficiency of killing enemies from great distances. That, in turn, made war zones more dangerous than in the past and added another reason for military personnel to stay in trenches as much as possible. Concealed snipers on both sides were constantly watching enemy positions and looking for chances to shoot soldiers who carelessly exposed themselves to enemy fire.

Artillery

DESPITE THE surprising importance of machine guns in the war, artillery guns were arguably the most important weapons used in the ground war. Ironically, their importance was magnified by the need to counter the defensive strength of machine guns themselves. Primarily offensive weapons, artillery comprised all types of large-bore guns that required crews to operate them, including cannons, howitzers, and mortars (see Glossary). They fired much larger shells than rifles and machine guns did and over greater distances. They could be fired from fixed platforms, mobile carriages or vehicles including trains, or from the decks of ships.

Artillery weapons go far back in time, to catapults used long before gunpowder was invented. Throughout history, however, their basic purpose changed little: to pound enemy positions as attacking armies advanced. Defending armies have used artillery guns as well, but artillery is most useful for breaking down defensive strongholds.

The artillery of World War I benefited from important recent innovations. For example,

breech-loading mechanisms enabled more rapid firing. Rifled barrels increased accuracy. Hydraulic recoil systems kept guns from moving from their fixed positions when they fired, thereby eliminating the age-old problem of having to re-aim guns after every shot. One of the best guns used during the war was the famous French 75 (named for its 75-millimeter-caliber shell). It could fire 16 rounds per minute without having to be realigned.

Guns also became lighter for the sizes of shells they fired and were easier to move and handle. Some guns also grew much larger. The bigger guns could fire heavier shells over greater distances. Toward the end of the war,

British artillery guns pounding German lines.

Collier's New Photographic History of the World's War (New York: P. F. Collier & Son, 1918)

Germany was using gigantic cannons to fire shells at Paris from distances of more than 60 miles.

Accuracy was also improved by technologies permitting the construction of shells that would behave more predictably when they fired. Improved accuracy and firepower made modern artillery yet another contributor to the perils of combat, as artillery fire was more likely than ever before to hit its targets. Moreover, shells were likely to come in larger numbers.

Improvements in modern artillery were especially important in the naval war. Since the invention of cannons centuries earlier, naval combat had revolved around ships firing big guns at each other. As recently as the early 19th century, naval cannon fire was so inaccurate that ships had to get as close as possible to enemy vessels to have a chance of inflicting serious damage with their nonexplosive cannon balls. Over the ensuing century, naval guns—like land guns—became more accurate and capable of firing farther. By the start of World War I, the biggest naval guns could shoot so accurately over long distances that a battleship could conceivably sink an enemy ship before it even realized it was in danger.

Getting through barbed wire entanglements was difficult in itself. The real danger was being shot while doing it.

Collier's Photographic History of the European War (New York: P. F. Collier & Son, 1917)

Barbed Wire

IN 21ST-CENTURY terms, barbed wire would be considered an example of "low technology," in sharp contrast to the higher forms of technology employed in other innovations discussed in this chapter. It is, however, an impressive example of the huge impact the simplest kind of technology could have on warfare.

Barbed wire consists of nothing more than two strong strands of ordinary metal wire,

about the thickness of a heavy pencil lead, coiled around each other, with sharp points (barbs) projecting at intervals. It was invented by Americans during the mid-19th century to provide cheap fencing around cattle ranches. During the Spanish-American War (1898), Theodore Roosevelt's Rough Rider cavalry unit used barbed wire to protect their camps in Cuba. The wire was used more extensively in the Russo-Japanese War (1904–1905). The most extensive use of barbed wire in warfare, however, occurred in World War I.

In the stagnant conditions of the western front, barbed wire was an ideal material for protecting trenches from enemy attacks. The methods used for stringing wire varied greatly, but its purpose was essentially the same everywhere: to stop enemy troops from penetrating defensive positions. Wire entanglements were typically erected far enough in front of trench lines that any enemy troops who reached the wires could not throw grenades over them into the trenches.

The wires themselves were fixed to posts in both regular and seemingly haphazard arrangements. Tautly strung wires would trip approaching soldiers, and loosely strung wires would tangle around anyone who fell into them. As attacks were often mounted in the dark, the wires were difficult to see. Animals had even more trouble than humans seeing them,

and the wires were particularly dangerous to horses. Horses falling into barbed wire were often seriously injured in their efforts to free themselves. Barbed wire was thus another innovation that contributed to the end of cavalry.

Poison Gases

ALMOST CERTAINLY the most notorious new weapons of the war were the poison gases used by both sides. They represented the first truly large-scale form of chemical warfare. Most of the approximately 20 different gases developed during the war were designed to kill victims who inhaled them, but each had unique properties and effects.

The three most commonly used gases were chlorine, phosgene, and mustard gas. Chlorine was the first lethal gas used in combat on the western front. It had a corrosive effect on human lungs that quickly killed anyone who inhaled much of it. It caused long-term congestive disorders in those who survived it. Phosgene was another gas that had a lethal corrosive effect, and it also irritated skin tissue.

"Mustard gas," the most notorious chemical weapon of the war, was actually not a gas. It was an atomized liquid that induced severe blistering externally and internally and caused painful vomiting and very slow death. Odorless and colorless, it was difficult to smell or see.

Because it was a liquid, it lingered on clothing and other surfaces and caused problems for anyone who later touched it. A peculiar and dangerous aspect of it was that people exposed to it typically noticed no ill effects from it until as long as 12 hours later. By then, it was too late to do anything about it.

While chemists on both sides of the war worked to create ever more lethal gases, others sought ways to protect people against their effects. The most effective solution was the gas mask, which soon became part of every sol-dier's kit. Early models were little more than chemically treated cloths used to cover one's mouth and nose. Gradually, more complicated and effective masks were developed. Fitting masks on faces posed problems. An American private recalled:

One never saw soldiers with beards in this war. The face must be clean shaven every day so that the gas mask would fit tightly around the face. A stubble of whiskers would allow the poison gas to penetrate the

Aerial view of clouds of poison gas spreading out.

Collier's New Photographic History of the World's War (New York: P. F. Collier & Son, 1918)

mask.... A daily shave was a military order. When in combat this is not an easy thing to obey, but we managed somehow. There were many times when I shaved in a half cup of coffee, after drinking the first half.

Eventually, all masks covered entire faces and contained glass eyepieces for seeing. Special masks were even made for dogs and horses. In fact, horses were considered so valuable that one American soldier said, "We were told of the value of horses, how scarce they were, and informed that a horse was worth four men. Our government could get a soldier by sending out a post card, but the procurance of a horse was not such an easy task. So, in case of a gas attack, the mask was first to be put on the helpless animal." Putting masks on the animals was not easy, however, so the soldiers were inclined to ignore that instruction.

Most gas masks worked simply by filtering the air users inhaled. The challenge was to develop filters that worked for the wide variety of gases troops might encounter. The masks saved many lives, but they were cumbersome to wear and made breathing, seeing, and handling weapons more difficult. An American artilleryman recalled that

gas mask pains and miseries begin to drive you wild. The straps on your ears
make them burn and sweat and itch—the tension on your forehead and temples is a perfect ache producer—the eye pieces cloud up and keep you wiping—the gas comes thru and stings a bit—so that your eyes smart and water, while your nose runs and you want to sneeze. But sneeze you dare not, for the reaction is invariably a gasp, and you're likely to get a lungful if you risk it.... After half an hour, the temptation to pull the blamed thing off, and take a chance on the gas being gone, is almost too great to resist.

Despite differences among gases, all had in common the property of being heavier than plain air. Consequently, they dispersed close to ground level and collected in whatever pits and depressions or trenches they reached. The simplest way to disperse gases against enemies was to open their containers on the ground and allow natural winds to blow them toward enemy positions. That procedure presented an obvious danger: if the wind shifted, it could blow the gas back onto the people releasing it. Handling poisonous gases was not a duty that soldiers welcomed. Strong winds could also lift gases into the sky and allow them harmlessly to disperse above their targets.

The first nation to use lethal gases as weapons during the war was Germany. After having

Make a Model Gas Mask

AN EASY WAY to experience what it feels like to wear a gas mask is to make a simple model mask. You can use the design on this page to design your mask.

Materials

- ✪ Pencil
- ✪ Cardboard
- ✪ Scissors
- ✪ Clear cellophane of any color
- ✪ Ruler
- ✪ Adhesive tape
- ✪ Bubble Wrap with small bubbles
- ✪ Elastic band or heavy rubber bands

Use a pencil to copy the mask design onto a piece of cardboard or heavy card stock, matching its labeled dimensions. Use scissors to cut out the eye and mouth holes, and then cut around the outside edge of the mask.

Cut two cellophane circles slightly larger than the eye holes and use adhesive tape to attach them to the back of the holes on the same side of the mask on which you have drawn its outline.

Make the air filter for the mouthpiece by cutting a strip of cardboard 2 inches wide and at least 11½ inches long. Bend the strip to form a cylinder, with its ends overlapping slightly. Place tape on the inside of the cylinder to hold the ends together.

Next, cut two circles of Bubble Wrap with slightly longer diameters than that of your cylinder. Attach each circle to one end of the cylinder with tape. Place the completed mouthpiece over the front of the mask and tape it in place from the backside.

Make a strap for the mask from a piece of an elastic band about 6 inches long and tape its ends to the edges of the mask just outside the eye holes. If you do not have a suitable elastic band, tie several strong rubber bands together and use them instead.

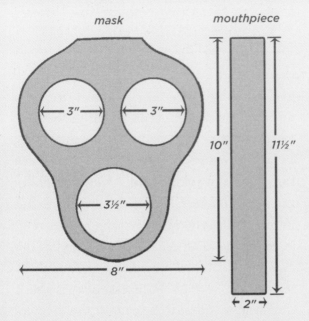

While wearing your model gas mask, keep in mind that real World War I masks were much heavier and more uncomfortable. When you walk around with the mask on, try to imagine what it was like wearing a mask while marching or fighting in the war.

American soldiers learning how to use gas masks in France.
Keystone View Company

limited success with gas on the eastern front, Germany released 168 tons of chlorine gas along four miles of French trench lines in Belgium in April 1915. Within minutes of engulfing 10,000 bewildered French Algerian troops in green clouds, the chlorine killed about half of them. Another 2,000 men who became disoriented and temporarily blind were easily taken prisoner.

Poisonous gases earned a terrible reputation during the war but ultimately accounted for only a small fraction of total casualties on both sides. As the war progressed, defenses against gas improved greatly and reduced casualties even though gas attacks steadily increased. By the end of the war, gases were largely ineffectual weapons. An immeasurable impact of poison gases, however, is their psychological effect on soldiers in war zones. So long as soldiers knew sudden gas attacks were possible, they could never relax and allow their gas masks out of their sight. They could not sleep in their trenches without wondering if they might never wake up.

In 1925, poison gas was outlawed in war by an international convention. Italy used poison gases in its invasion of Ethiopia in 1936, but they were never used in the second world war. Nevertheless, the combatant nations in that war stockpiled deadly gases for possible use and kept supplies of gas masks ready in case their enemies suddenly used them.

Tanks

GAS-POWERED AUTOMOBILES and trucks were products of late-19th-century innovations in internal-combustion engines. Although still in their infancy when World War I began, they were sufficiently developed to make important contributions to modernizing the warfare. They greatly increased the speed and efficiency with which personnel, supplies, and messages could be moved. They moved faster and carried heavier loads than animal-drawn wagons and carriages, and they required less care. Nevertheless, they were not yet ready to displace horses and other animals altogether. Dependent on decent roads, they often could not go where animals could, especially in the muddy and broken terrain of the western front. Then midway through the war, an entirely new kind of motorized vehicle was introduced.

If there was one innovation that was uniquely a product of the first world war, it was the tank. Tanks are heavily armored and self-propelled combat vehicles that move on endless loops of metal belts known as "caterpillar tracks." No earlier war had ever seen anything quite like them. When the war began, no one was even thinking about inventing such a vehicle. Tanks were conceived only after the stagnant battlefield conditions created by trench warfare made it essential to find a means of breaking out of the stalemate. British army officers began discussing the idea of armored vehicles with caterpillar tracks as early as autumn 1914.

The idea of armored war vehicles was not new. What was original about tanks was their being self-propelled and their riding on caterpillar tracks similar to those used on farm machinery. Caterpillar tracks offered several notable advantages over wheels. Because they ran the full lengths of their tanks, they distributed the tanks' weight evenly, making it easier to avoid getting stuck in mud and holes. They also provided far better traction because the metal blades on their tractor belts pulled against every object they touched. Tanks would also eventually have the ability to move their left and right tractor belts at different speeds

HOW TANKS GOT THEIR NAME

With the Royal Navy behind the development of British tanks, it is not terribly surprising that one of the first names the navy gave them was "landships." The early tanks did, after all, have characteristics resembling those of naval warships. In early 1916, the project developing the tanks gave them the code name "water tanks." Eventually, the armored vehicles became known simply as "tanks."

British light tank of 1918 with turret action and high speed

British tank of the earliest type

German land battleship captured in 1918

Improved French tank first used in 1918

Francis A. March, *History of the World War* (Chicago: United Publishers, 1919)

and in opposite directions, allowing them to make quick, pinpoint turns and even to turn completely around in small spaces.

Tanks were expressly designed to overcome the conditions that had been making mobile warfare impossible in western Europe. They could glide over muddy, pockmarked terrain; climb up and down steep grades; push through barbed wire barriers effortlessly; and even roll directly over wide trenches. In short, they offered to restore mobility to battlefields. Like any complex new inventions, however, their early models had serious limitations.

In early 1915, Winston Churchill, then still first lord of the British Admiralty, began pushing his government to support development of an armored vehicle that could move through trenches and overcome machine gun emplacements. An army engineer drafted a list of specifications for such a vehicle. It included all the capabilities mentioned above, plus the capability to carry a 10-man crew, a field gun, and two machine guns. Such a vehicle had the potential of becoming an extremely powerful offensive weapon.

The British army was initially not interested in Churchill's proposal, so the Royal Navy took up the challenge. By September 1915, its first tank was ready for testing. It performed poorly, but a much improved model dubbed the Mark I was ready a year later. Almost 50 of them

made their first battlefield appearance on the Somme in September 1916. The lumbering 30-ton tanks were so slow they could barely keep up with foot soldiers. They were operated by very inexperienced crews and had a regrettable tendency to break down. Nevertheless, their heavy armor made them nearly invulnerable to machine gun bullets.

A British infantry corporal recalled his surprise at seeing the tanks when they appeared the first time: "We were all absolutely flabbergasted. We didn't know what to think. We didn't know what they were because we hadn't been told anything about them. It was an amazing sight. . . . They scared the guts out of the Germans. They bolted like rabbits."

Throughout the remainder of the war, the British made their tanks lighter, faster, more maneuverable, and more reliable. By the end of the war, the British put more than a thousand tanks into combat. Meanwhile, the French were developing tanks of their own, independently of the British developments. Tanks helped the Allied war effort but did not achieve the great breakthrough that Churchill had wanted. Despite improvements in their design and construction, they remained too slow, too unreliable, and too few in number to turn the tide on the western front.

Germany never had the same interest in tanks during the war that the Allies had.

They developed only one model. It was huge, comparatively fast, and heavily armed, but it was not ready until near the end of the war and was not built in large numbers. Ironically, Germany would be the leading proponent of tanks during the second world war. In that war, vastly improved tanks would play decisive roles on almost every front.

Telecommunications

TELECOMMUNICATIONS, OR the transmission of messages over long distances by technological methods, took a great leap forward during the mid-19th century with the invention of the telegraph. That innovation made possible virtually instantaneous transmission of coded electric messages through wires. The next great leap occurred during the 1870s with the invention of telephonic voice transmissions over wire. Both telegraphs and telephones found important military uses almost as soon as they were invented, and both were important in World War I.

Communications with trench systems on the western front were maintained through elaborate networks of mostly underground telegraph

Allied soldiers repairing field telephone lines in the midst of a gas attack.

and telephone lines connecting units. Keeping these networks in operation was an ongoing challenge because lines were often broken by artillery shells.

The next advance in telecommunication was the invention of wireless radio transmission during the first decade of the 20th century. World War I was the first war to employ that revolutionary new method of communication. However, because radio was still in its infancy in 1914, there were serious limitations to its uses. For example, it was then essentially a wireless form of telegraphy. Radio was useful for coded transmissions but not for voices. The most outstanding problem with primitive radio equipment, however, was its size and weight. Radios were too big and heavy to be easily portable. Early reconnaissance airplanes, which would have benefitted most from radio communication, were too small and weak to carry radios. Thus, although radio technology existed, reconnaissance pilots communicated their observations to their bases by such unlikely means as wrapping messages around rocks they dropped from the sky and tying messages to the legs of homing pigeons.

One of the most valuable uses of radio during the war was in communicating with ships at sea. For the first time in history, warships sailing at immense distances from their home bases could coordinate their operations with up-to-the-minute instructions from their bases and with other ships out of their line of sight.

Radios also proved useful for communicating with troops in the field. However, with radio such a new technology, it was natural that military units using the devices would make dangerous mistakes. One of the most common radio mistakes made during the war was sending messages containing important military intelligence and forgetting that enemies could be listening, too. The Russians were particularly prone to sending uncoded messages that gave the Germans information they used to their advantage.

Eventually, all sides learned that radio transmissions must be coded. That development led to yet another—the specialized art of code breaking.

6

THE WAR AT SEA

THE YEARS LEADING up to the outbreak of World War I saw massive buildups of modern battleship fleets in many of the world's navies. When the war finally began, it was naturally expected that powerful new battleships would meet in epic fleet actions similar to those of the Napoleonic Wars a century earlier. To almost everyone's surprise, however, the great new battleships saw little action and faced each other in only a few, inconclusive battles. The real naval war was not between rival warships but between warships and enemy merchant ships.

Meanwhile, something else equally unexpected was happening. The most important vessels of the war proved to be not battleships but submarines. This was especially surprising because before the war began, few people even imagined submarines could become effective weapons in war. Another unexpected turn in the war

69

was the growing importance of airplanes in naval operations. When the war began, few people suspected airplanes would ever become weapons. By the end of the war, however, several nations were building aircraft carriers to extend the war in the air out to sea. This development pointed the way to the central importance of air power in 21st-century navies.

The importance of World War I's naval phase is best understood by considering what each navy's objectives were. Throughout history, navies have played important roles transporting troops to assaults on enemy territories. With the notable exception of the Allies' Gallipoli campaign, however, the first world war saw few such naval actions. The navies' main objectives during the war were to disrupt enemy shipping while protecting their own nations' shipping. Great Britain and Germany depended especially heavily on foreign trade to feed their peoples and supply their industries. Trade disruptions seriously weakened them.

The naval phase of World War I offers more examples of how warfare can be slow to catch up with advances in the military technology it employs. The modern, diesel-powered ships navies had built up before the war were so unlike ships of the previous century that no one was sure how to use them. When reliable ocean-going submarines were developed, even naval leaders were unsure what to do with them. Not only did few people think they might be valuable weapons, many thought using underwater weapons against enemy ships would be both sneaky and unethical—like shooting someone in the back.

Naval Warfare in History

THE INDUSTRIAL Revolution of the 19th century brought many changes to naval warfare. From around 1850 to 1914, naval ships underwent greater transformations than had been seen throughout the previous 2,000 years. These changes occurred faster than navies could learn how to master them. Wooden sailing ships at the mercy of tides and weather gave way to much larger, steam-powered iron ships that could ignore most natural conditions. Like the artillery weapons of land forces, ships' guns also grew bigger and more deadly. Muzzle-loading cannons of old sailing ships could batter wooden vessels until they sank, but they were slow to load and difficult to aim. Even the biggest could not hit targets more than about a mile away. Moreover, the only directions in which they fired was directly off the sides of their ships. Because the maneuverability of ships was at the mercy of current and wind, ships needed skilful handling merely to get their guns in position to fire.

The late-19th- and early 20th-century advances in ship design and artillery went well beyond increases in size and strength. Steam- and diesel-powered engines allowed ships to move faster and to maneuver more easily than sailing vessels ever could. Moreover, their breech-loading guns could fire farther, faster, and more accurately than old cannons could, and their shells exploded on contact. Unlike old cannons, modern guns were mounted on turrets that could be individually rotated to fire in almost any direction. This innovation went back to the US Civil War, in which the Union Navy's famous ironclad *Monitor* was the first ship to have its cannons mounted on a turret.

By the start of World War I, the biggest guns on battleships could fire shells weighing many hundreds of pounds as far as 20 miles. Indeed, they could fire shells so far their targets could not be seen from the decks of their ships because they went beyond the visible horizon. All these improvements came with a price: enemy guns could do the same things.

Approaching World War I

As ADVANCES in ship design and weaponry were modernizing navies, rivalries among the European nations intensified. By the turn of the 20th century, the great powers of Europe were engaged in an arms race similar to the future "missile race" of the mid- to late-20th-century Cold War. Before 1914, the focus was on how many battleships each nation had. In 1906, this competition escalated when Great Britain launched the HMS *Dreadnought*, the first battleship armed entirely with big guns. Earlier battleships carried both large and medium-size guns designed to fire over different distances. Traditionally, gunners honed in on targets by noting where their misses struck water. For example, when shells fell short of their targets, gunners made adjustments to fire farther. Having different-size guns on a ship made it difficult for spotters to tell which shell splashes were associated with which size guns. Using guns of the same size eliminated that problem.

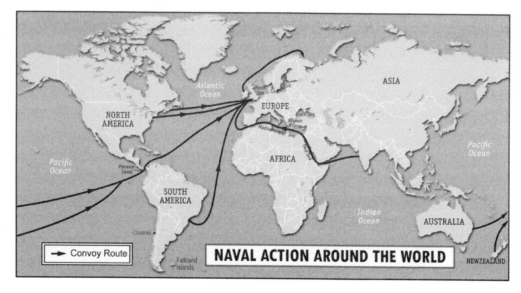

NAVAL ACTION AROUND THE WORLD

There was also another reason for making all the guns big. When properly handled, the biggest guns could sink or disable enemy vessels before they got near enough to bring smaller guns into play. After 1906, all major navies rushed to build their own *Dreadnought*-type battleships. Soon, the word "dreadnought" itself became synonymous with all-big-gun battleships.

For centuries, Britain's Royal Navy had been undisputed master of the seas. Public pressure within Britain to maintain naval superiority was strong. Although Germany had only recently been unified as a nation, it was Europe's greatest land power in 1914. The country had only a brief naval history, but during the decades leading up to the war, it invested heavily in building its own modern navy under the leadership of Admiral Alfred von Tirpitz. Other European nations naturally wondered why Germany needed such a powerful navy. Because Germany lacked a worldwide empire as extensive as that of Britain or France, its navy could have been built for only one reason—to challenge Britain's mastery of the world's oceans. Watching Germany's naval buildup motivated Britain to make its own Royal Navy even stronger.

By 1914, virtually all sizeable navies of the world—including several South American navies—were adding dreadnoughts and super dreadnoughts to their fleets. Public attention to these developments created the expectations that battleships would play a prominent role in World War I. That never really happened, however. After investing so much money and energy in building up their battleship fleets, governments were hesitant to risk sending them into combat. A ship that could sink an enemy 20 miles away was a valuable weapon—but perhaps too valuable to risk having it sunk by enemy guns firing from the same distance.

Kaiser Wilhelm II exercised personal control over Germany's naval strategy. He took

German battleship squadron exercising on the North Sea before the war.

great personal pride in the 27 modern battleships and battle cruisers in Germany's modern High Seas Fleet. Germany's navy was not quite as large as Britain's, but its ships were arguably superior. Nevertheless, Wilhelm was reluctant to risk losing his ships in combat and rarely allowed them to sail far from their home ports. Needless to say, the ships' officers and crews became frustrated by the lack of action they saw during the war. That frustration would lead to surprising consequences toward the end of the war.

Naval Strategies

ALTHOUGH ALL the major powers involved in the war entered it with substantial naval forces, most major fighting involved only British and German warships. As the map of western Europe shows, Germany's only sea routes to the rest of the world were through the North Sea, which was partially blocked by the British Isles. Sailing surface ships through the narrow and closely guarded English Channel would have been nearly impossible. The only alternative was to sail north and go around Scotland. That was not easy either, as the Royal Navy's main base, Scapa Flow, was at the northern end of Scotland.

To prevent the Germans from reaching the Atlantic Ocean, the Royal Navy blockaded their ports and kept a squadron of cruisers patrolling the frigid waters connecting the Atlantic with the North Sea. During the last year of the war, British and American naval vessels laid nearly 70,000 mines between northern Scotland and Norway to seal off escape from the North Sea.

Britain's North Sea strategy throughout the war was simple: to blockade German ports to prevent both military and merchant ships from entering or leaving. That strategy worked well. As the war progressed, Germany steadily ran short of both raw materials to supply its wartime industries and food to feed its people. By the end of the war, its military was running out of supplies and the entire nation was close to starvation. In wartime conditions, Germany simply could not produce enough food to feed its own people. The eventual Allied victory thus owed as much to its naval success as it did to its armies on the ground.

Germany would have liked to pursue a similar naval strategy against Great Britain, which was even more dependent on overseas trade. However, blockading British ports was impractical. Aside from the difficulty of sending surface ships through the British blockade, Britain had ports on more seacoasts than could be easily contained. Germany soon adopted another strategy by turning to its underwater navy—its submarines.

Fighting at Sea Begins

WHEN THE war opened in early August 1914, most German warships were still in their home ports. Some were at sea far from home. The number of German vessels at sea was small, but because they posed serious threats to Allied shipping, the Royal Navy made hunting them down a priority. The British chased two German battle cruisers all the way across the Mediterranean Sea. They thought they had the enemy vessels trapped in the Aegean Sea, but the Germans surprised them by entering the then-neutral Turkish port of Constantinople. After the Turkish government bought the ships from Germany, the cruisers entered the Black Sea, where they harassed Russian shipping.

Meanwhile, near the other side of the world, Germany's Far East Squadron off the coast of China barely escaped an encounter with British and Japanese warships on August 6 and fled east, across the Pacific Ocean. Under the command of Admiral Maximilian von Spee, the squadron attacked Allied island bases. On November 1, the squadron met a British squadron and sank two of its battle cruisers off the coastal Chilean town of Coronel. Emboldened by this success, von Spee took his squadron around Cape Horn to look for British warships in the South Atlantic. Before sailing, however, he told a German friend

in Chile he felt "quite homeless.... I cannot reach Germany; we possess no other secure harbour; I must plough the seas of the world doing as much mischief as I can, till my ammunition is exhausted, or till a foe far superior in power succeeds in catching me." His last words were prophetic.

With the British public outraged by the disastrous Battle of Coronel, the British government sent a powerful squadron south to find von Spee. On December 8, the British got their vengeance when the Royal Navy surprised the German ships while they were taking on coal in the Falkland Islands. Before the German ships could put out to sea, they were overwhelmed by British guns, which sank four of them. Von Spee himself died in the action. The only German ship to escape from the Falklands was destroyed several months later.

Battles in the North Sea

LATE AUGUST 1914, the end of the first month of the war, saw the first North Sea action between British and German ships, which met off Germany's Bight of Heligoland. After the Royal Navy sank four German cruisers, Germany became more cautious about sending ships into the North Sea. In late September, however, a single German submarine sank three British cruisers off the coast of the Neth-

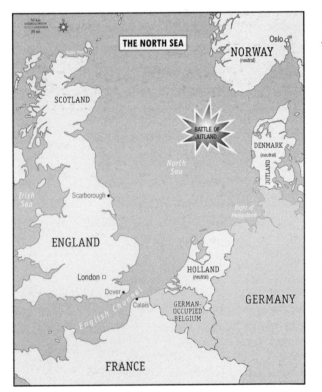

erlands in one hour. Over the next few weeks, German submarines made additional successful attacks close to Britain. These surprising developments shocked both the British and the Germans and signaled how dangerous submarines could be as offensive weapons.

In mid-December, the British received another shock when a German battle cruiser squadron bombarded several coastal towns in northeast England, including Scarborough, causing 500 civilian casualties. Unaware the entire German High Seas Fleet was trailing the squadron, the British force sent in pursuit missed an opportunity for a major battle. In late January, the Royal Navy had a more successful encounter in the same region with another German cruiser squadron, driving it off after inflicting heavy casualties. Afterward, naval action in the North Sea quieted down for more than a year.

At the end of May 1916, Germany's High Seas Fleet and Britain's Grand Fleet finally met head-on in an encounter known to the Allies as the Battle of Jutland, after the name of a nearby Danish peninsula. Germans named it after the nearby Strait of Skagerrak. The 260 ships of the combined fleets were more numerous than those of any other naval battle in modern history. It is a record unlikely to be broken. If another epic naval battle ever occurs, it will likely be decided by missiles and airplanes launched

from small numbers of ships that will never even be in sight of each other.

The Battle of Jutland began after most of Germany's High Seas Fleet entered the North Sea from the Baltic, hoping to surprise British cruisers off the Norwegian coast. The German navy was hoping to do enough damage to the British fleet to break Britain's blockade. The British had more ships, but the German ships were stronger and had better guns.

Tipped off by intercepted radio messages, the British sent the Grand Fleet down from Scapa Flow to meet the Germans, and other squadrons joined in support.

Despite the huge numbers of ships involved, Jutland was not a colossal battle. Afraid of encountering unseen mines and submarines, the commanders of both fleets were hesitant to commit their most valuable battleships to attacking. After the fleets maneuvered around

British admiral John Jellicoe.

Library of Congress LC-DIG-ggbain-29932

Battle of Jutland Warships (not including submarines) (lost vessels in parentheses)		
Class	**British**	**German**
Dreadnought battleships	28 (0)	16 (0)
Pre-dreadnought battleships	0 (0)	6 (1)
Battle cruisers	9 (3)	6 (1)
Armored cruisers	8 (3)	0 (0)
Light cruisers	26 (0)	11 (4)
Destroyers	78 (8)	72 (5)
Totals	149 (14)	111 (11)

U-BOATS

German submarines were known to the Allies as "U-boats," after their German name, *U-Boots*, short for *Unterseeboots* (undersea boats). At the start of the war, Germany had fewer than 30 U-boats, to which it added about 80 new boats per year throughout the war. Submariner duty was dangerous. More than half of all U-boats were lost in action during the war. Nevertheless, U-boats sank more than 5,000 Allied and neutral ships.

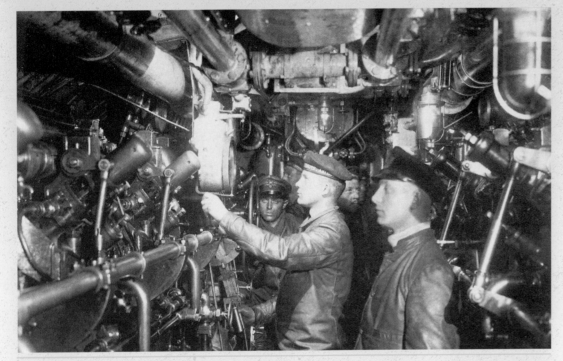

The cramped engine room of a German submarine.

for several hours seeking favorable positions, a small number of ships on each side fired at each other. The German commander, Admiral Franz von Hipper, soon correctly sensed his force was outgunned and began to withdraw. The British commander, Admiral John Jellicoe, tried to cut off the German retreat but gave up the effort as darkness and mist reduced visibility.

Only about 10 percent of all the ships and men had actually been involved in fighting. After the smoke from the ships had cleared and the fleets had tamely returned to their home ports, the Germans were found to have lost 11 ships and 2,500 men. The British had lost 14 ships and about 6,000 men. Because of its lighter losses, Germany celebrated a victory at home. Statistically, at least, it had won the battle. In reality, however, Britain had won the day. The British losses were numerically inconsequential, but British sailors were greatly disappointed. The day after the battle, a midshipman wrote a letter stating, "Our one desire is to meet the enemy once more on his own ground and under any conditions, our only stipulation being that the visibility and the disposition of our Battle Fleet will force him for the first and last time to accept a general action which can and will be fought to a finish."

The important result was that the Royal Navy forced the German surface ships out of the North Sea, ending German hopes of sending its great fleet into the open seas.

From that moment, Germany relied mostly on a policy of unrestricted submarine warfare against all shipping even suspected of aiding the Allies. It would, however, repeatedly reverse itself on that policy until the United States finally became fed up with German attacks on its ships and declared war on Germany in early 1917.

Meanwhile, the British navy was digesting an important lesson it had learned during the Battle of Jutland. The heavy armor protecting the sides of its great warships was of little use against big guns firing shells so high in the sky that they came down and penetrated the ships' decks and destroyed gun turrets. It was clear that decks and turrets had to be greatly strengthened. This was another dramatic change from 19th-century warships.

Submarines

THE MOST surprising naval development of the war may have been the crucial role submarines eventually played. Although almost unknown in previous conflicts, submarines were not a recent invention in 1914. The first submarines were developed during the late 18th century, and a one-man submersible vessel was even used in the American Revolu-

tion. During the US Civil War, a Confederate submarine named the *Hunley* sank a steam-powered Union ship blockading the harbor of Charleston, South Carolina. Hand-cranked by its crew, the *Hunley* sneaked up on the ship and rammed a "torpedo" attached to the end of a spar into it. After releasing the spar, the sub backed away before the torpedo exploded. Soon afterward, the *Hunley* itself mysteriously sank. Submarine technology had a long way to go, and the *Hunley*'s fate did not win submarines many supporters.

Making submarines practical military weapons awaited the development of steel hulls, electrical motors and battery systems for underwater propulsion, and gas or diesel engines for surface propulsion. They had to operate safely in the open sea and be able to fire self-propelled torpedoes from underwater. By the early 20th century, submarines were being successfully propelled by diesel engines on the surface and by battery power underwater. All major navies were adding submarines to their fleets, but these vessels saw little combat before World War I began. Russia tried using submarines during its war against Japan in 1904–1905 but with little effect. During one of the Balkan Wars, a French-built Greek vessel became the first submarine to fire a self-propelled torpedo at an enemy ship—but it missed. It was not surprising that when World

German U-boat stranded on the southern coast of England.

War I began a few years later, no one thought much of submarines.

When a single German submarine sent three British cruisers to the bottom with their entire crews in September 1914, the British sailors could scarcely have understood what had hit them. After the role of the submarine in the sinkings became known, British ships hesitated to enter the North Sea, in which growing numbers of German subs were operating. To make those waters even more dangerous, both the Germans and the British laid down extensive underwater mine fields. While the British essentially cleared the North Sea of German surface vessels, the waters surrounding the British Isles remained extremely dangerous to Allied shipping.

After Germany's early sinkings of British warships, German submarines had little success against Allied warships. Virtually blind when they operated underwater, the subs had to do most of their sailing on the surface and were much too slow to keep up with surface ships. The only way they could pose a serious threat to enemy warships was by surprising them in traps. As their limitations became evident, Germany turned to using them mainly against merchant vessels.

In February 1915, Germany announced to the world it would use its submarines to sink all vessels carrying war materials to the Allied Powers. At first, its submarines followed the recognized international rules of naval warfare by stopping ships, inspecting their cargoes, and allowing passengers and crew to take to lifeboats if the ships' cargoes proved to be carrying war materials. However, as merchant ships carrying hidden guns began fighting back, submarine commanders became less considerate. They began sinking suspect enemy ships on sight to avoid being sunk themselves.

As the war progressed, losses of Allied shipping to German submarines grew ever larger. Germany set a goal to destroy so many merchant ships carrying goods to Britain that it would starve Britain into dropping out of the war. Eventually, British shipping losses grew so numerous that it appeared Germany's goal might be realized. Germany's success, however, was coming at a cost. While it was fighting the Allies with guns and torpedoes on land and on sea, it was also fighting a propaganda war. Its ruthless war on merchant shipping was sinking many ships from neutral nations, including the United States, that Germany did not want to offend.

The *Lusitania*

ON MAY 7, 1915, Germany scored a small tactical success that became a public relations disaster. On that date, one of its submarines sank the British ocean liner *Lusitania* off the coast of southern Ireland. More than 1,000 civilian passengers, including more than 100 Americans, died when the ship went down. The public outcry in Britain and the United States was great. The fact that the *Lusitania* was carrying war materials made it a legitimate military target, but that information was not known to the public. Nevertheless, killing a large number of citizens of a powerful neutral nation was a blunder that turned American public opinion strongly against Germany. US president Woodrow Wilson sent a strong protest message to the German government but resisted pressures to declare war on Germany. As Germany did not want the United States to enter the war on the side of the Allies, it temporarily pulled back on its policy of submarine warfare. The United States would not declare war on Germany for another two years, but the *Lusitania* sinking contributed to that decision.

The numbers of ships sunk by U-boats steadily increased through 1916, but the Allies replaced their losses so fast that the German strategy was not achieving its desired effect. The Allied blockade on Germany, however, was working very well. The country was running out of food and raw materials, and the possibility of Allied armies breaking through the stalemate on the western front was growing greater. By the end of 1916, Germany's leaders concluded that desperate measures

The sinking of the *Lusitania* served as a powerful Allied rallying cry against Germany.

The day before the *Lusitania* sailed from New York City, the German government published this ad in American newspapers.

Frank N. Simonds, *History of the World War* (New York: Review of Reviews, 1919)

were necessary to avoid defeat. In late January, Kaiser Wilhelm accepted a plan to resume unrestricted naval war at a higher level with the goal of starving Britain into submission within six months. The prospect of drawing the United States into the war was very high, but Germany's naval leaders were confident they could help end the war before American forces could arrive in Europe in strength.

The US Navy in the War

LIKE MANY European nations, the United States had greatly strengthened its own navy in the years leading up to the war. With long Pacific and Atlantic coastlines and growing overseas trade to protect, the United States had recognized the importance of having a strong naval force since its Civil War. During the late 19th century, the federal government had invested heavily in the building of powerful, modern ships. Some of these new ships were used to crush a Spanish fleet in the Spanish-American War of 1898. In late 1907, President Theodore Roosevelt sought to impress the world with American naval might by sending a fleet of 16 battleships on a well-publicized cruise around the world. This "Great White Fleet," as it came to be known because its ships were painted white, demonstrated the modernity and strength of the US Navy and its ability to go anywhere in the world it was needed.

By 1907, Britain's recent creation of the first dreadnought battleship had rendered the ships of the Great White fleet nearly obsolete. The US Navy moved to correct that problem by ordering more modern ships. Meanwhile, the fleet's 14-month-long cruise taught the navy a great deal about ship design and handling that was put to use in the building of more powerful ships in the dreadnought class before World War I.

By the start of the war, the United States trailed only Britain and Germany in the size of its naval force. In 1914, the US Navy had about 300 ships of all types, including 17 pre-dreadnought class battleships and 10 modern dreadnoughts. Although the United States did not enter the war until 1917, it continued its vigorous shipbuilding program. Before the war ended, the navy added another six dreadnoughts, but most of its shipbuilding program went into smaller vessels, such as merchant ships, destroyers, and antisubmarine craft. Thanks to American industrial might, the country was turning out more than 100 new ships per month by the end of the war. By then, the navy had expanded to more than 1,000 vessels. The US Navy has since remained unchallenged as the most powerful naval force in the world.

Despite its great power, the US Navy played only a minor role in World War I itself. By early

1917, when the United States formally entered the war, the only serious threat posed by enemy navies came from German submarines, against which America's great battleships were largely useless. Most of the biggest US Navy ships stayed close to home, while its destroyers and antisubmarine boats went to work with the Allied navies in the North Atlantic, North Sea, and the Mediterranean Sea. Another major task of the US Navy was to protect convoys of American soldiers transported to Europe.

Confident that its submarines would sink most of the troopships carrying American soldiers to Europe, Germany was not greatly concerned about American entry into the war. Henning von Holtzendorff, head of the German Admiralty Staff, went so far as to tell the kaiser, "I give your Majesty my word as an officer, that not one American will land on the Continent." His prediction was off the mark. As things turned out, some American troops did lose their lives to German submarines, but more than two million eventually reached France safely. Germany's greatest naval weapon thus failed completely when it was most needed.

Happy American sailors returning home from Europe aboard the USS *Texas*. Now a floating museum anchored near Houston, the *Texas* is the last surviving dreadnought battleship.

7
THE WAR IN THE AIR

LIKE THE NAVAL phase of World War I, the air war brought surprises. Chief among them was the fact there even was an air war. When the war opened in 1914, few people expected airplanes to play any kind of combat role. Planes had been invented barely a decade earlier, and most were so small and flimsy they could barely carry a single person, let alone a dangerous weapon. At best, they were expected to be useful for high-altitude reconnaissance but not much more. Instead, airplanes underwent rapid developments and emerged from the war as the military weapons of the future.

Within only four years, military aviation forces grew from handfuls of slow, fragile little airplanes to large squadrons of fighter planes and strategic bombers. By the end of the war, naval forces were building aircraft carriers to extend the air war to the sea. These impressive developments increased the human death toll

during the war, but they also benefitted non-military aviation. The war helped make all airplanes stronger, faster, more reliable, and safer. It also created thousands of skilled pilots, aeronautical engineers, and aircraft mechanics and raised public interest in aviation. The war made few positive contributions to human progress; aviation was one of them.

Although powered airplanes were a very recent invention, aviation itself was not new. Hot air balloons large enough to lift humans into the sky had been used since the late 18th century. They could travel great distances but only in directions the wind carried them. By the beginning of the 20th century, lighter-than-air aviation technology had greatly advanced. Airships enclosing huge gas-filled balloons within rigid, cloth-covered frames were soon making controlled human flight possible for the first time. Using engine-powered propellers for propulsion, the airships were called dirigibles because their movements were directable. Both heavier-than-air and lighter-than-air craft would have important reconnaissance and combat roles in the war.

Seen as one of the most glamorous duties in the military, aircraft piloting appealed strongly to young men. In *Sagittarius Rising* (1936), his wartime memoir, Cecil Lewis wrote that Britain's Royal Flying Corps (RFC) "attracted the adventurous spirits, the devil-may-care young

bloods of England, the fast livers, the furious drivers—men who were not happy unless they were taking risks."

The same could be said about the pilots of every nation in the war. The first American killed in combat in the war was Edmond Genêt, a pilot flying for the RFC. Before he was shot down, he wrote a letter to his mother in which he said, "I'd rather die as an aviator over the enemy's lines than find a nameless, shallow grave in the infantry."

Reconnaissance

RECONNAISSANCE, OR reconnoitering, is the gathering of information through observation. Military forces have always sought to collect as much reliable information as possible about their enemies. They want to know where their enemies are, where they are going, how large their forces are, and what weapons they have. During World War I, gunners firing artillery shells needed spotters to tell them where their shells were falling so they could adjust their aim as necessary.

A century ago, no one even imagined the electronic technologies that now make things such as radar and global positioning systems (GPS) possible. Modern technology makes it relatively easy to know exactly where one's own and enemy forces are deployed. Without such tools, however, the only way World War I military personnel knew where enemies were positioned was for observers to spot them with their own ears and eyes.

Binoculars and telescopes naturally helped in reconnaissance, but even they were not much use when lines of sight were blocked by forests, buildings, mountainous terrain, bad weather, smoke, or other obstacles. Smoke was a particular problem in naval combat because ships of that era belched out so much thick, black smoke they often could not see each other.

The best observation points in any war are typically the highest places spotters can reach, such as the tops of hills, trees, and buildings. The advantages aviation offered to reconnaissance should be obvious. Hot-air balloons were used for high-altitude observation as early as the US Civil War. Much greater use was made of balloons for the same purpose in World War I.

During the first world war, most observation balloons were inflated not with hot air—which requires a continually burning flame to keep its trapped air warm so it stays expanded—but with hydrogen gas. Much lighter than air, hydrogen is plentiful and easy to collect but is also highly flammable and thus dangerous. Helium gas, which is now used in balloons and blimps, is almost as light as hydrogen and is much safer

to use because it is chemically inert and will not burn. Helium is abundant in the universe, but on earth it is rare. Processes for extracting it were not efficient during the early 20th century, so balloons and dirigibles had to use flammable hydrogen. Serving on observation balloons and dirigibles was inherently risky. Hydrogen's flammability made such service so dangerous that British soldiers called the men who went up in balloons "balloonatics."

From Reconnaissance to Aerial Combat

BEFORE 1914, no one seriously imagined what would later become known as fighter planes. At that time, none of the nations involved in the war had anything remotely like an air force. In fact, none of them had many airplanes of any kind. However, because airplanes offered such obvious advantages as reconnaissance tools, the various armies quickly began acquiring and using them for that purpose.

It is important to appreciate how feeble those first military airplanes were. At best, they could carry a pilot and an observer who

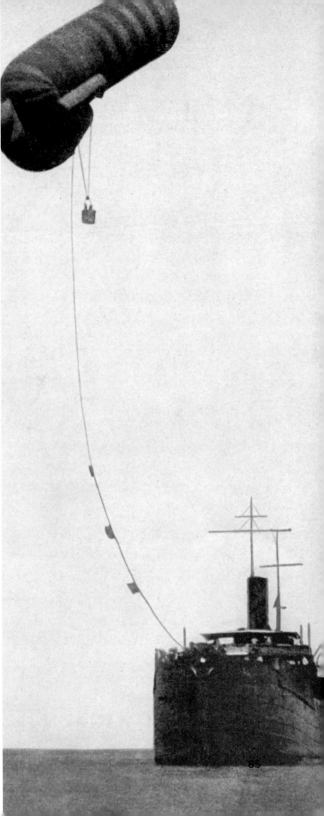

Like their land-based counterparts, observation balloons tethered to ships greatly extended naval forces' reconnaissance capabilities.

Collier's New Photographic History of the World's War (New York: P. F. Collier & Son, 1918)

photographed troop positions. At worst, they could carry only a lone pilot, who either struggled to operate a camera while trying to control his plane or relied on his memory to report what he saw on the ground. Despite these limitations, the value of aerial reconnaissance soon became evident in the contributions it made in ground actions such as the Allied victory in the First Battle of the Marne.

As planes assumed greater roles in reconnaissance, they could cover more ground than observation balloons could and could even fly directly over enemy positions. They were limited, however, in how they could report their observations to ground bases. Radio transmitters were too heavy and bulky to fit on small planes, so pilots had to either land to make their reports or write them down and drop them from the sky in canisters. Sometimes they even used pigeons to deliver their reports.

As airplanes and photographic equipment improved and pilots and observers grew more experienced, aerial reconnaissance took on ever greater importance. One drawback was that advances that benefitted one side in the war also benefitted the other. While armies worked to develop their reconnaissance planes, they also looked for ways to prevent enemy planes from observing them. Shooting the planes down from the ground was not practical with the guns available at the start of the war. The alternative was to try to shoot the planes down from the air. Meanwhile, both sides worked to develop ground-based antiaircraft weapons.

During the early months of the war, enemy pilots often acknowledged each other with a friendly wave when they passed in the sky during their reconnaissance flights. Soon, however, that chivalrous behavior gave way to pilots attacking one another. At first, they threw things such as bricks and grenades at each other—usually without effect. Then they took pot shots at each other with rifles and pistols. Hitting a moving target with a single shot or two while piloting a plane was nearly impossible. About the only effect was to encourage enemy pilots to shoot back. That naturally dented the notion that all pilots belonged to some kind of gentlemanly brotherhood. Their gloves were off, and their aerial encounters soon became much nastier.

To hit a fast-moving target in the air, the most obvious type of weapon to put on airplanes was a machine gun that could fire continuous streams of bullets. Mounting machine guns on early planes presented several problems, including the guns' size and weight. Mounting them so they could be aimed at enemy aircraft was another problem. The most desirable direction in which to aim a gun then was directly in front of the pilot. Unfortunately, that direction sent bullets into propellers, and some pilots actually shot the propellers off their own planes—with predictable results. Some pilots put metal flanges on the propeller blades for protection against bullets. That technique added unwanted weight and subjected pilots to the danger of being hit by ricochets.

A daring French pilot named Roland Garros attached steel plates on his plane's propeller, confident that if he could fire his machine gun directly ahead for a few seconds, enough bullets would go through the propeller to down an enemy plane. When he was warned he would destroy his own propeller in the process, he coolly replied, "Ah, so what. I will make a glide landing. If I stay over French-held territory, I've got no problem. The cost of a propeller against the wiping out of a German plane and its crew." Garros enjoyed spectacular success. In April 1915, he shot down five enemy planes in a few weeks. After his sixth kill, however, his engine failed, forcing his plane down behind enemy lines.

Wanting to know the secret of Garros's success, the Germans sent his plane to Berlin. There, Anton Fokker, a Dutch aircraft maker, examined the plane. He pronounced Garros as having been incredibly lucky not to be hit by a ricochet and came up with an entirely new idea: a timing mechanism that synchronized machine gun firing with propeller movement. That allowed pilots to fire machine guns di-rectly through propellers with no risk of hitting them, regardless of engine speed. For almost an entire year, Fokker's invention gave German pilots a huge advantage over French and British pilots, whom they shot down at alarming rates. During that period, the life expectancy of Allied pilots serving on the western front was measured in days. Sometimes pilots newly assigned to squadrons were killed before they even unpacked their kits in their new quarters. Eventually, however, the Allies figured out how to duplicate Fokker's invention and neutralized the German advantage.

By 1916, both sides in the war were building new and better planes as fast as they could to replace the increasing numbers of planes being shot down. At that stage of the war, almost the only reason fighter planes existed was to shoot down other fighter planes. They were of little use against ground targets. Behind their fighting, however, remained the urgent need for planes to continue their reconnaissance missions.

French-built Nieuport fighter plane with both a drum-fed machine gun and belt-fed machine guns synchronized with its propeller.

Collier's New Photographic History of the World's War (New York: P. F. Collier & Son, 1918)

Flying Aces

As AERIAL combat grew more frequent, a new class of skilled fighter pilots developed. These were the elite pilots who squeezed every ounce of speed and maneuverability out of their planes to put themselves in the best positions

The Red Baron.

Edward Rickenbacker.

to shoot down enemy aircraft. Pilots who shot down at least five enemy planes were dubbed "aces." To help raise morale both within the military and at home, many air services created special awards to recognize their ace pilots.

The most successful and famous fighter pilot of the war—and probably of all wars—was Germany's Manfred Freiherr von Richthofen. He was better known as the "Red Baron" after he started flying a bright red triplane in early 1917. He had begun the war as a cavalry officer and switched to the German air service in 1915. Some aces used acrobatic flying techniques, such as daredevil loops, to get behind enemy planes. Richthofen preferred simpler, more cautious tactics, such as flying very high and then diving steeply at an opponent from the rear, with the sun behind him. He also liked to fly with other pilots covering his flanks and rear. His excellent marksmanship, piloting skills, and intelligent tactics allowed him to shoot down more planes than any other ace in the war. He was credited with 80 confirmed kills before he himself was shot down in April 1918. Ironically, the bullet that killed him came not from an enemy plane but from a gun (possibly a machine gun) on the ground. Though mortally wounded, he landed his plane safely on the ground moments before he died. He was not quite 26 years old.

The top American ace in the war was Eddie Rickenbacker, who scored 26 air combat victories. He got a late start in the fighting because he did not join the US Army until the United States entered the war in early 1917 and was not allowed to fly in combat until April 1918. He scored his first victory only eight days after the Red Baron was shot down. In contrast to Richthofen, who was actually younger than he was, Rickenbacker lived to the age of 82 and enjoyed a long career in aviation.

As aerial combat became more frequent, pilots flew more frequently as members of squadrons than as individuals. When they met enemy squadrons, large battles in the sky often ensued, giving rise to the term "dogfights." In contrast to the aerial battles of future wars, the airplanes of World War I flew slowly and could make sharper turns than faster planes. This made it possible for enemy planes to get very close to one another and put on spectacular air shows. Cecil Lewis described dogfighting in *Sagittarius Rising*:

When a number of machines had closed and were engaged in a "dog-fight," it was more a question of catch as catch can. A pilot would go down on the tail of a Hun, hoping to get him in the first burst; but he would not be wise to stay there, for another Hun would almost certainly be on his tail hoping to get him in the same way. Such fights were really a series of rushes, with momentary pauses to select the next opportunity—to catch the enemy at a disadvantage, or separated from his friends.

Thanks in part to the fame garnered by aces such as Richthofen and Rickenbacker and the drama and excitement of aerial dogfights, fighter piloting was popularly perceived to be glamorous. When pilots were not flying, they lived in comfortable quarters that were usually away from danger, and they dined well. Their lives contrasted starkly with those of the infantry troops living in squalid trenches. The reality was somewhat grimmer. Most pilots were lucky to survive more than a few weeks of combat, and their deaths were usually anything but glamorous.

Observation Balloons

WHILE AIRPLANES were playing rapidly increasing roles in the war, lighter-than-air craft were also advancing. Observation balloons were used by all participants throughout the war. They were even used on seagoing ships, which benefitted from their being able to spot enemy vessels far over the horizon that were not visible from lower altitudes.

The wireless radio technology used during the war did not lend itself well to voice transmissions. Radio messages could be sent in Morse code but took much longer to transmit than voice communications conveying the same messages. Radio equipment was also too heavy to work well in small aircraft. Because observation balloons were tethered to the ground or to ships, they could easily be wired with telephones. This made it possible for the observers manning them to speak directly to ground- and ship-based command centers with no delays.

Artist's rendition of a dogfight in which a British biplane is shooting down a German Albatross.

Francis A. March, *History of the World War* (Chicago: United Publishers, 1919)

Spotter suspended from an observation balloon using a telephone to help direct artillery fire.

Frank N. Simonds, *History of the World War* (New York: Review of Reviews, 1919)

Shooting down observation balloons was one of the earliest combat roles for fighter planes and continued to be important throughout the war. Because the balloons were tethered, they made nearly stationary targets, and their gas bags often erupted in flames when they were hit. When observers suspended in baskets below the balloons saw enemy planes approaching, they had no way to lower their balloons, so they had to get to the ground on their own—either by sliding down lines or jumping out, while ground crews scrambled to pull the balloons down before enemy fire ignited them. The observers often used parachutes to bail out.

Zeppelins

ONE OF the most frightening developments of the war was the use of huge airships to bomb civilian areas. Most major participants in the war had their own great airships, but the unrivaled leader in that technology was Germany's Graf (Count) Ferdinand von Zeppelin, whose name came to be a synonym for giant airships. His interest in airships went back to the US Civil War, which he had witnessed as an official observer. Seeing how balloons were used for reconnaissance in that war made him think about the possibilities of building lighter-than-air ships that could be used for controlled flight.

He began building his first airships around the turn of the 20th century and persuaded the German government to subsidize his work.

At the start of the war in 1914, the German navy had some zeppelins in service and began adding more, as did the German army. Because they could fly higher and farther and carry heavier loads than the airplanes of their time, zeppelins had many potential military uses. In January 1915, Germany started sending them on night bombing runs against England. For the first time since the 11th-century Norman invasions, inland communities in England experienced the direct threat of foreign attacks. A German newspaper reveled in the idea that "London, the heart which pumps lifeblood into the arteries of the degenerate huckster nation," was being "mauled and mutilated with bombs by brave German fighting men in German airships." Most zeppelin raids did little serious damage, but they had a strong psychological effect on the public. British civilians could no longer feel completely secure in their own beds. The zeppelin attacks were a harbinger of much worse things to come from the sky during the second world war.

Despite their formidable size—the length of several football fields—zeppelins had several limitations that made them vulnerable to airplane attack. They were slower than airplanes, large and easy to spot, and prone to exploding

Make a Parachute

PARACHUTES WERE FIRST imagined during the Renaissance by Leonardo da Vinci and others of his time, but no human used one until the late 18th century. World War I saw their first military applications. Initially, they were used mostly by crews of observation balloons. Observers worked in baskets suspended below the balloons, which were tethered to the ground. After around the midpoint in the war, when the balloons were threatened by enemy aircraft, the observers used parachutes to jump to safety. Meanwhile, ground crews furiously winched the balloons to the ground before they could be shot at.

Most airplane pilots were not issued parachutes until later in the war. The delay was partly due to the need to avoid adding extra weight to the earliest planes. It was also partly due to a concern that pilots might use their parachutes to abandon their planes too quickly when they were damaged. Whatever the reasons, many pilots who might have been saved by parachutes went down with their burning airplanes.

To appreciate how parachutes work, you can easily make a small one from a variety of materials. This activity suggests using a plastic bag, but a large sheet of strong tissue wrapping paper or even a large napkin can work well. Whatever materials you use should weigh as little as possible.

Materials

- ✪ Ruler
- ✪ Scissors
- ✪ Lightweight plastic bag
- ✪ Pencil or pen
- ✪ Sewing thread
- ✪ Adhesive tape
- ✪ Paper clip
- ✪ Small toy

Measure and cut a square at least 12 inches on each side from the thinnest plastic bag you can find. Fold the square in half two times and mark the midpoint of each unfolded side of the resulting smaller square. Draw a line connecting the two marks and cut across it to remove the unfolded corners. When you open the sheet, you should have a nearly perfect octagon.

Cut 8 pieces of thread each about 15 inches long. Use a pencil or pen to poke small holes near each corner of the octagon. Tie a piece of thread to each hole and use small pieces of tape to reinforce the corners.

Lay the octagon flat on a table and lift all the threads together above its center so each is the same length. Tie the ends of the threads in a simple knot and cut away the loose ends. Hook a paper clip over the knot and attach a small toy to it.

Test the weight of the toy by gently opening your parachute and dropping it from a standing position. If it falls too rapidly, try a smaller toy or other lighter object. When you find an object whose weight allows the parachute to fall slowly, look for higher places from which to drop it, such as an upper-story window, a balcony, or the top of a staircase with a banister. Be careful not to lean over from a high place, and avoid dropping your parachute on another person or a pet.

in flames when hit by the incendiary bullets used against them. Consequently, many of them were shot down, with their crews suffering horrible deaths in fires. The Germans tried to compensate for those handicaps by flying their zeppelins over England at altitudes too high for British planes to reach. The results, however, were disastrous. Unlike the aircraft of later generations, zeppelins lacked pressurized cabins to protect crews from the thin air of high altitudes. When they rose as high as 20,000 feet, their crews became dizzy and disoriented. Some crewmen in open-air gun mounts actually froze to death. In 1917, Germany gave up on using zeppelins as bombers. By then, it had airplanes to perform that function.

The Emergence of Bombers

AIRPLANES STARTED dropping bombs early in the war. Initial efforts, however, were merely individual pilots' crude attempts to drop random bombs by hand while flying reconnaissance missions. The development of real bombers awaited advances in aircraft and engine design that enabled construction of planes large and powerful enough to carry heavy loads over great distances. Germany was the first nation to build a successful heavy bomber, the Gotha. During the summer of 1917, it began sending squadrons of Gothas on daytime raids against targets in England from bases on the coast of Belgium. As had been the case with the first zeppelin raids two years earlier, the Gotha raids caused public panic.

Also as with the earlier zeppelin raids, the Gotha raids began losing their effectiveness as British air defenses improved. A key advance in neutralizing bombers of all types was the development of more effective antiaircraft guns.

One of Graf Zeppelin's great airships after landing in France the year before the war began.

Library of Congress LC-DIG-ggbain-12236

Even before the war, the British were developing antiaircraft shells designed to explode at fixed altitudes and spray shrapnel pellets in all directions. These had a devastating effect on the delicate fabrics enclosing the airships for which they were intended. They also could have a lethal effect on flimsy airplanes and pilots in open cockpits. They were not, however, very effective during the war because it was difficult for antiaircraft gunners to estimate the altitudes and speeds of their targets.

Naval Aviation

AERIAL WARFARE was not limited to land-based forces. The navies of most of the nations fighting in the war made pioneering contributions too, especially in the field of airships. In the naval sector of the war, aircraft were invaluable for spotting submarines. Those vessels actually spent a large majority of their time on the surface because they could operate underwater on battery power for only limited periods. Britain began employing airships to search for German U-boats in 1915. The limitations of airships motivated Britain to develop stronger airplanes to do the same job.

So long as naval operations remained close to coastlines, airplanes served well as recon-naissance aircraft. They lost their usefulness, however, when naval operations went beyond their flying range. The next challenge, therefore, was to find a way to carry airplanes farther out to sea. Planes that could land on water existed, but they could not land on rough seas and generally had difficulty taking off from water. Nevertheless, several navies adapted ships to carry airplanes out to sea. Some had short launching platforms from which the airplanes could take off. When the planes returned from reconnaissance work, they landed in the water close to their ships, which used cranes to hoist them back aboard. Needless to say, this was a perilous system, especially in the rugged North Sea, where the planes were most needed.

The next step in naval aviation was to build ships on which airplanes could both take off and land. In August 1917, an airplane made the first successful landing on the deck of a British ship that had been converted from a cruiser. The modern aircraft carrier was born. Carriers did not play a big role during the last year of the war, but they pointed the way to the future. By the early 21st century, airplanes and missiles would be the most important weapons of modern navies, which might now be said to be floating air forces.

Early attempt by a reconnaissance pilot to drop a bomb by hand.

Frank N. Simonds, *History of the World War* (New York: Review of Reviews, 1919)

British ship using a crane to lift a seaplane aboard. Note the ramp on which planes took off from the ship.

Collier's Photographic History of the European War (New York: P. F. Collier & Son, 1917)

8
ANIMALS GO TO WAR

ANIMALS HAVE ALWAYS been part of wars. They have served as food for troops, hauled weapons and supplies, borne soldiers into battle, carried messages, done sentry duty, helped find wounded soldiers, and raised troop morale as pets and mascots. World War I may well have been the war in which animals played the largest and most varied roles. Unfortunately, it was also probably the war in which the most animals died. Machine gun bullets, artillery shells, bombs, poison gases, barbed wire, harsh weather, food shortages, diseases, and brutal working conditions were as cruel to animals as they were to human beings.

Animals found their way into the war through several different routes. Many were conscripted at home to serve the needs of the military. These included horses, other draft animals, messenger dogs, and carrier pigeons. Others were farm animals, pets, and even

exotic zoo animals separated from their owners in war zones. They usually were drafted into service, ended up in dinner pails, or became pets and mascots. Some of their offspring were born in the war-torn trenches and knew no other life. Finally, there were wild animals of all types—birds, mammals, reptiles, amphibians, fish, and such invertebrate creatures as insects and spiders. Some of these creatures provided unwelcome company in trenches and camps, but a surprising variety of them were adopted as pets.

Animals made countless valuable contributions to the efforts of all the nations fighting in the war. Millions served, and some even received military commendations. Animals helped transport personnel, did much of the heavy labor that could not be done by men or machines, carried untold numbers of messages, and helped save thousands of human lives. They also served as loyal and affectionate companions to soldiers, sailors, and others starved for reminders of what life was like away from war.

Horses

THE ANIMALS most closely associated with wars have long been the horses ridden by the cavalry troops. The origins of modern cavalry tactics go back to the Middle Ages, when the invention of stirrups made it possible for riders to stay firmly on their horses' saddles while fighting. By the 19th century, cavalry units were vital parts of all European armies. They performed reconnaissance work, protected infantry troops on the march, and served as "shock

French cavalry troops watching one of the observation planes that was making cavalry reconnaissance work obsolete.

troops" that hit enemy forces hard enough to turn battles. Powerful horses allowed troops to charge into battles at crucial moments and put enemies to flight in ways that foot soldiers could not. When World War I began, the western European armies expected their cavalries to be as important as they had been in the past. About one-third of their regiments were cavalry, and they needed large numbers of horses.

As earlier chapters show, cavalry tactics proved to be almost useless on the western front. Because of their great size, horses made even easier targets for machine guns to hit than soldiers. While cavalry remained important on the eastern front and in the Middle East, most armies fighting in the west eventually gave up on cavalry and converted their cavalry regiments to other kinds of service, such as artillery support. Nevertheless, horses remained vitally important on the western front. They were still used for reconnaissance and for carrying messages. They were especially valuable, however, for pulling artillery guns and heavy supplies through muddy and irregular terrain where motorized vehicles could not easily go.

Future wars would have more versatile vehicles to do heavy carrying and pulling, but in the first world war, horses and their donkey and mule cousins remained vitally necessary to keep armies moving. Maintaining supplies of horses played a critical role in the outcome of the war. Horses suffered horrendous casualty rates. When they were not facing machine gun bullets, artillery shells, or poison gases, they were overworked, underfed, and weakened by punishing weather and diseases. Resupplying horses became increasingly critical to all the armies as the war progressed.

These horses pulling an Austrian army car through mud demonstrate their value on the western front.

Library of Congress LC-DIG-ggbain-18223

"OUR DUMB FRIENDS' LEAGUE"

A SOCIETY FOR THE ENCOURAGEMENT OF KINDNESS TO ANIMALS.

BLUE CROSS FUND
For WOUNDED HORSES
AT THE FRONT.
DONATIONS IMMEDIATELY TO—
ARTHUR J. COKE, Secretary.
58, VICTORIA STREET, LONDON, S.W.

Amid the terrible devastation of the war, organizations such as Britain's Our Dumb Friends League worked to alleviate the suffering of animals without regard to which side they belonged.

Caring for animals in combat areas was difficult, but their suffering did not go unnoticed. In a letter home, a British soldier said that one of the beastliest things of the war was "the way animals had to suffer. It mattered not to them if the Kaiser ruled the whole world; and yet the poor beasts were dragged into hell to haul rations and gear over shell-swept roads and field paths full of holes to satisfy the needs of their lords and masters." On one occasion, a British officer saw a soldier treating a wounded horse with such tender care he complimented the man on his compassion. The soldier replied, "Well, sir, how would you feel if you was both deaf and dumb and could not make known the pain you feel?"

Before the war, Germany was well supplied with horses, which it had been breeding for years. When the war began in August 1914, it immediately mobilized more than 700,000 horses for cavalry and other uses. Its ally, Austria-Hungary, mobilized 600,000 horses. As wartime conditions steadily reduced those numbers, Germany could not easily import more horses because of the British blockade of its ports. Instead, the Germans took all the horses they could seize when they occupied Belgium, France, the Ukraine, and other countries. Left with almost no horses to pull coal wagons in the winter months, Belgium consequently suffered serious fuel crises. Eventually,

Germany itself ran so short on horses it could not move its artillery and supply wagons easily on the western front.

Great Britain had far fewer horses than Germany when the war began but was better positioned to import more, mostly from the United States, Canada, Australia, New Zealand, and Argentina. The United States alone eventually exported more than 1 million horses to Europe. When American troops finally entered the war in 1917, they took almost 200,000 more horses with them. Only a few hundred of those horses would eventually return home. Their losses had a damaging effect on American agricultural productivity.

Incomplete records make it difficult to know how many horses served in the war, but estimates have run as high as 8 million, most of which died. Perhaps one-quarter of the horses that died were killed in combat. The rest succumbed to disease, starvation, and sheer exhaustion. Many even drowned in deep mud after falling down when they were too weak to get up again. In the unsanitary conditions prevailing on the western front, horses were ravaged by equine flu, infected fly bites, ringworm, anthrax, and other ailments. Injuries, especially from contact with barbed wire, caused additional problems.

Feeding and caring for horses were constant burdens to armies throughout the war. Horses ate 10 times as much as humans did, and virtually all their fodder had to be imported and carried to the front. In fact, fodder for horses may have accounted for the bulk of supplies shipped to the front. The United States was a major supplier of animal fodder, and all its exports had to get past German submarines to reach Europe. Germany had even greater problems feeding its horses. Occasionally, it was reduced to mixing sawdust in fodder. Not surprisingly, hundreds of thousands of German horses died from starvation.

The contributions of horses to the war were not all positive. Horses also aggravated the many health problems already distressing troops. Soldiers, especially those from farms, typically enjoyed having horses around, and the animals helped keep up morale. At the same time, however, the horses made the bad sanitation situations in the trenches even worse. The vast piles of manure they created attracted disease-carrying insects, and the rotting bodies of dead horses piled up faster than they could be buried.

World War I would be the last major war in which horses would play an important role. Changing military technology made cavalry obsolete in European wars, and its role would be assumed by tank corps in future land wars. Horses themselves would not become entirely obsolete, but most of their other functions would be taken over by other motorized vehicles and self-propelled artillery weapons.

Dogs

THE NUMBERS of dogs serving in the war were only a fraction of the numbers of horses that served. Dogs, however, were far more versatile and had many valuable functions. They are best known for carrying messages in war zones, but they also did extensive work as sentries and guards, helped locate wounded soldiers, carried small supplies through difficult terrain, and killed rats that infested the trenches. Some performed such heroic feats in combat they were decorated for their bravery.

Breeds used in the war were mostly medium-sized dogs whose colors blended into the surroundings, making the dogs difficult for enemies to see. They included bloodhounds, bulldogs, collies, fox terriers, German shepherds, retrievers, and sheep dogs. Using dogs in the war was not a haphazard business. Most European armies had special units for training and handling them. Germany alone put more than 30,000 trained dogs into service, and France had about 20,000. When American soldiers arrived in 1917, they brought no trained dogs with them but borrowed some from the French and British. Both sides in the war retrained dogs captured from the enemy to serve them.

Dogs made almost ideal message carriers on the western front. They were smart, fast, agile, and reliable and were difficult to spot from a

Animals, like humans, needed protection against poison gas.

SERGEANT STUBBY AND RAGS

Several dogs performed such outstanding feats of heroism that they became famous. One of the most celebrated was an American dog known as Sergeant Stubby. A stray that may have been a pit bull terrier mix, he was adopted as a mascot by soldiers training in Connecticut before being posted overseas. One of the soldiers, Robert Conroy, smuggled Stubby on the troop ship carrying him to France in 1917. Over the next 18 months, Stubby lived in the trenches through countless battles and offensives. All the while, he helped keep up the morale of troops around him while mastering skills that helped save lives. For example, he learned to warn of approaching gas attacks and incoming artillery shells. On several occasions he located wounded soldiers in no-man's-land and once single-handedly trapped a German trying to infiltrate Allied lines.

When the war ended, Robert Conroy smuggled Stubby back to the United States. There the famous war hero marched at the head of parades, met US presidents, and became the mascot of the Georgetown University football team. He also received many other honors, including a gold medal from the Humane Education Society presented to him by General John J. Pershing, who had commanded the American Expeditionary Force in the war. He lived until 1926.

Another heroic dog named Rags had a story similar to that of Sergeant Stubby. An American army private named James Donovan found Rags abandoned in Paris and took him back to his infantry unit. While performing the dangerous work of stringing communication lines on the front, Donovan trained Rags to carry messages attached to his collar. In July 1918, Donovan and Rags were in an infantry unit that was cut off and surrounded by Germans. Thanks to a message Rags carried back to his base, an artillery barrage and reinforcements saved the unit. Rags was credited with helping to save 42 lives.

Rags continued to carry important messages and was also skilled at warning soldiers of incoming artillery fire. He helped save more lives until both he and Donovan were badly wounded in October and sent back to the United States together. Donovan died shortly after the war ended, but Rags lived until 1936 and enjoyed the same type of celebrity that Stubby had experienced.

distance when they were running. They were especially valuable in situations when telephone lines failed and carrier pigeons were not suitable. Carrier pigeons could carry messages faster than dogs, but they were limited to returning to their home bases and were thus essentially one-way messengers. In contrast, dogs could be trained to carry messages in multiple directions. Properly trained messenger dogs could get messages through almost any type of terrain. On many occasions, dogs delivered messages that saved numerous human lives.

Dogs trained to work with Red Cross personnel also helped to save lives. In addition to carrying medical supplies on their backs, these dogs knew how to locate wounded soldiers and bring help to them. Sometimes, the dogs were known to drag wounded soldiers to safety.

Sentinel dogs helped protect camps and trenches by giving advance warnings of approaching enemies. Thanks to their more acute senses of smell and hearing, dogs made better sentries than humans in some ways. Some learned to warn of incoming artillery shells when they heard high-pitched sounds inaudible to human ears. It is possible that sentinel dogs saved even more lives than messenger and Red Cross dogs.

Among other duties performed by dogs were carrying supplies and pulling carts and small weapons. Some of the larger breeds pulled machine guns and mortars when troops were on the move.

Carrier Pigeons

SOME PIGEON breeds have strong homing instincts that make them ideal message carriers. For reasons not fully understood, these pigeons can be taken far from their home cotes, or coops, to unfamiliar locations, released, and almost unfailingly find their way home. During the Franco-Prussian War of 1870, the French made extensive use of carrier pigeons to deliver microfilm messages to Paris while it was surrounded by Prussian armies.

In World War I, much greater use was made of carrier pigeons. Around 100,000 pigeons eventually served in the war. Every army had a special pigeon division within its signal and communications branch. Using mobile pigeon cotes to establish home bases for the birds, these divisions gave baskets of pigeons to units going into battle or starting special missions. If the units were unable to communicate with their bases by telephone, they attached written messages to the legs of pigeons and released them to fly home.

About 95 percent of all messages sent by pigeons during the war are estimated to have arrived safely. In addition to instinctively knowing how to find their way home, pigeons made nearly ideal messengers because they could fly as fast as 50 miles per hour and were so small they were difficult to see and even more difficult—but not impossible—to shoot down. One of the few ways to bring down a flying pigeon was to set a hawk or falcon on it, but that was not a practical solution in a war zone.

Pigeons were not used merely by army units. They also helped save many lives when they were used to carry distress signals from ships torpedoed by U-boats. Before radio equipment became more portable, reconnaissance pilots occasionally used pigeons to send messages while they were flying. Improved radio communications would eventually make carrier pigeons obsolete in war but not for many years after World War I. During World War II, the British alone used more than 250,000 pigeons to carry messages.

Like war dogs, carrier pigeons produced some heroes. The most famous was Cher Ami, which British pigeon breeders gave to the US Army Signal Corps in France. Cher Ami earned renown for helping to save an American infantry battalion cut off and surrounded by Germans during the Battle of the Argonne in October 1918. When this so-called Lost Battalion also came under misdirected Allied artillery fire, it sent out three messages by pigeon to notify its base where it was. The first two pigeons were shot down by the Germans. Cher

Even when released from the dark interior of a tank, with no idea where it was, this pigeon probably delivered the message it was carrying.

Train a Dog to Carry Messages

THE DOGS USED as messengers during the war learned their skills through careful training before they went into service. Their training usually began in simple surroundings that were gradually made more difficult until they resembled war zone conditions. You can begin training a messenger dog in the simple conditions around your home or in a park.

Materials

- Dog that likes both you and a friend
- Dog collar
- Pouch or small bag to attach to the collar
- Paper and pen or pencil
- Dog treats such as biscuits
- Friend to serve as an assistant

Attach a small pouch or paper bag to the collar on your dog. Write a message on a piece of paper. Let your dog see you place it and a dog treat inside the pouch. This will tell the dog its mission is beginning. Have your friend run at least 20 yards away. Release the dog and shout "Take message!" as your friend calls for the dog to come. When the dog reaches your friend, the friend should detach the pouch, remove the treat from it in view of the dog while praising it, and give the treat to the dog.

Repeat the entire procedure as many times as it takes for the dog to deliver its message without being called. Increase the friend's distance from your starting point each time. As your dog gains confidence, have your friend go to a place out of direct sight. With repeated practice, your dog should learn to carry messages to your friend without being called. With further training it can learn to carry messages to specific people you name.

If you train your dog in a public place, be sure not to violate local leash laws.

Ami delivered the third message, and the battalion was saved.

What made Cher Ami's feat impressive was not merely the fact the bird got through, but also the circumstances in which the bird did it. Like the first two pigeons, Cher Ami was shot down. A bullet went through one of its legs and its breast and blinded it in one eye. Despite its horrible wounds, Cher Ami managed to take off again and complete its mission. Veterinarians worked feverishly to save its life but could not save its leg, so they gave it a wooden replacement.

After the war, Cher Ami was taken to the United States triumphantly and given many honors. In June 1919, it died from its battle wounds. It was then stuffed and mounted on permanent display in the Smithsonian Institution's National Museum of American History, where it can still be seen. Until its death, Cher Ami was believed to be a male pigeon, but when a taxidermist worked on its body, it was found to be a female.

Other Animals

HORSES, DOGS, and pigeons were merely the most numerous and best known of the many species of animals that served during the war. Donkeys, mules, oxen, and even cattle were also used extensively to pull weapons and carts.

When the Germans were running low on draft animals, they briefly used zoo elephants to pull loads. In the desert fighting in the Middle East, camels were used extensively as cavalry mounts because of their great tolerance for hot, dry conditions. The Allies shipped several hundred camels to Southwest Africa to assist the South African campaign against that German colony.

One of the most surprising uses of animals occurred in the Royal Navy. British submarines kept white mice because they could smell dangerous gas fumes before humans could. The alarmed squealing of the submariner mice saved more than one submarine crew from disaster. Mice and canaries were also commonly used by "miners" on the western front who dug deep tunnels under enemy trenches to plant explosives. Both creatures were useful for warning of the presence of dangerous gases.

Pets and Mascots

THE WAR'S most interesting animals may have been the pets and mascots that servicemen kept. Some servicemen smuggled animals from home with them when they were posted abroad, but more often they acquired pets they found in the places where they were serving. Dogs and cats were always welcome among troops. Germany's ace fighter pilot, the

Red Baron, kept a beloved pet dog with him at his bases. In the trenches, cats were especially welcome. Content to stay close to their new owners, they did not require much troublesome care. They made themselves even more welcome when they waged war on the rats that infested the trenches. Dogs could be fine rat catchers, too. A British officer writing home told about the little canine mascot his regiment had adopted at his training camp:

It has gone with the regiment everywhere they went. It is a mascot. There are a dreadful lot of big rats here so the dog is getting very fat. You see, it eats so many rats. Soon it will get so fat it will not be able to catch any more rats. Then it will not get enough to eat so it will get thin again. And then it will be able to start catching more rats and get fat again.

On the western front the bulk of the fighting occurred amid agricultural areas. Thousands of pets and farm animals got loose when farms were destroyed, and they fled to escape the fighting. Some large farm animals were taken into military service. Others were taken into field kitchens and eaten. Many farm animals were adopted as pets, even those that might have made tasty meals. In general, however, farm animals suffered terribly on the western

British naval officer checking his submarine's white mice.

Frank N. Simonds, *History of the World War* (New York: Review of Reviews, 1919)

Write a Letter Home from the Western Front

LIVING AS THEY did among unrelenting death and destruction, soldiers often found themselves fascinated by the natural beauty of plants and wildlife struggling to survive amid the general desolation. Many trench soldiers filled their time by writing letters home to their families and sweethearts. Because they generally had little news to report or did not want to tell about the horrible things they experienced, they tended to write about more pleasant things. An American officer who censored his men's letters described them as pathetically cheerful: "They do not know where they are, or have any idea of what is going to happen to them. They write very cheerful letters, but they are so inarticulate, and express so little, or rather so inadequately, the love which the men feel; but I hope the wives and mothers can read between the lines, as I can who know the circumstances." Many soldiers wrote about things such as flowers, wild animals, butterflies, and pets.

Materials

✪ Writing paper
✪ Pen or pencil

Imagine you are a soldier or nurse on the western front and write a letter to someone important to you at home. Pick any kind of animals you wish to write about, so long as you might actually encounter them in the trenches. They might be stray dogs, cats, or wild animals you have adopted as private pets; animals adopted as company mascots; or wild animals you simply observe from a distance.

Think about how being in the midst of the war might affect your feelings toward the animals you write about. For example, would you feel more kindly disposed toward a mouse raiding your trench than you would toward a mouse invading your own home? Would a pet dog mean more to you at the front than at home? Would you take greater interest in observing butterflies in the trenches than you normally do? Try to get inside the heads of people serving on the front to understand why animals were important to them.

front. Only about one in 20 of the animals survived the war.

In December 1915, a unit of British soldiers in the trenches eagerly looked forward to making a Christmas dinner of two fat geese. Instead of cooking and eating the geese, however, the men decided the personable birds would make wonderful mascots and skipped their Christmas feast. The reprieved geese remained with the unit throughout the war, constantly entertaining the men and lifting their morale. After the war, they were taken to England. One lived until 1920, the other until 1931.

Many servicemen craved the affectionate companionship of pets they had enjoyed at home and eagerly adopted stray cats and dogs they encountered. Often they found that the animals were equally eager for human companionship, and strong bonds were formed. A British army chaplain who found a kitten in the crater of a dugout hit by an artillery shell wrote that if anything speaks of home, it is a kitten: "It carries our memory back to the blazing fire and the cat sleeping within the fender.... The crater belongs to war; the kitten to peace. The one speaks of death; the other of life."

War zone pets were not, however, limited to cats and dogs. Most types of farm animals became pets and mascots. Donkeys, geese, goats, pigeons, pigs, and rabbits were all popular among troops.

Servicemen also made pets of many wild animals they encountered. Mice were popular, but their larger and more vicious cousins, rats, were not. The only pleasure soldiers got from rats was in organizing competitive hunting events to go after them. Some soldiers tamed foxes and kept them as pets. One fox that became the mascot of a British air squadron spent a lot of time flying. Turtles and frogs were also popular pets.

The strangest animals to find their way into the trenches were exotic creatures from zoos disturbed by the war. Animals in zoos in or near war zones may have suffered even more than farm animals. Many depended on exotic foods that could not be imported during the war and starved to death in their enclosures. Others were killed by local government authorities to avoid their endangering people if enemy bombs allowed them to escape. Some zoo animals nevertheless ended up as pets and mascots. They included monkeys and chimpanzees, lion cubs, and at least one full-grown bear and an Australian emu.

Members of the Australian Expeditionary Force with their British bulldog mascot.

Photos of the Great War: World War I Image Archive

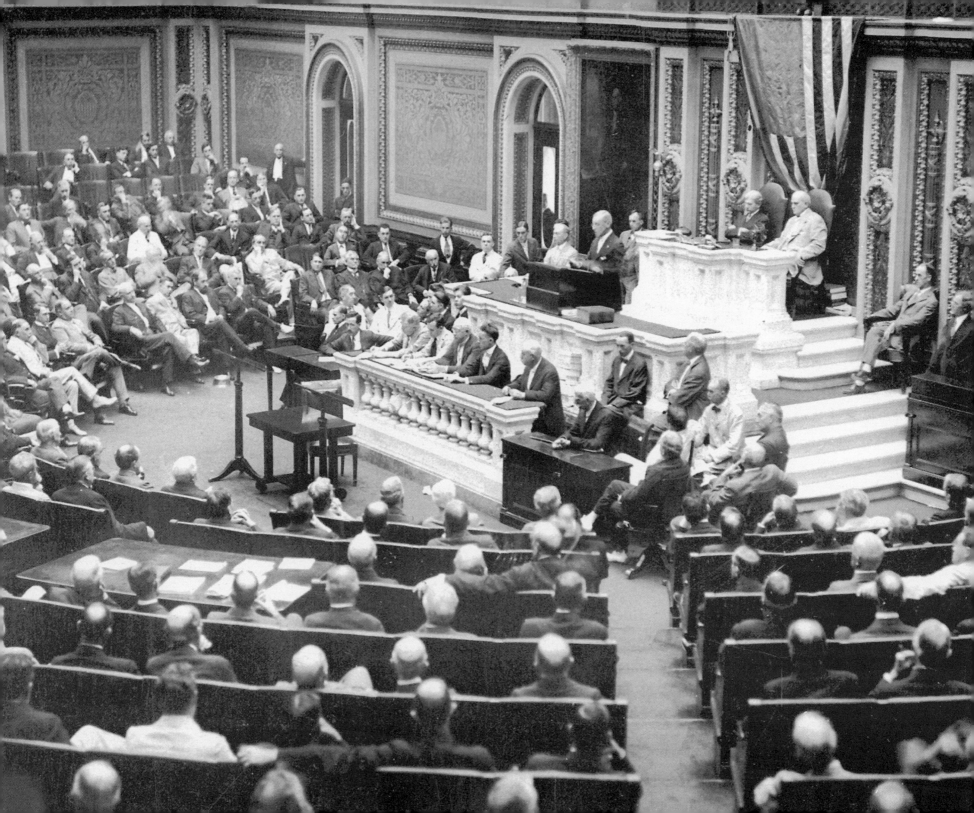

9

ENTER THE UNITED STATES

WHEN THE UNITED States finally declared war on Germany in early 1917, World War I was already two and a half years old. American involvement in the war did not begin then, however. During its years as a neutral power, the United States had supplied large quantities of vital materials to the nations fighting in the war. At the same time, thousands of individual Americans had joined Allied services to help fight.

Many American pilots were already flying combat missions for British and French aviation units. Some were looking for adventure. Others volunteered out of a sense of duty. When the war ended, Bogart Rogers, who had flown for Britain's Royal Flying Corps, wrote to his fiancée, "Thank goodness I've seen a bit of the world and taken a chance. At least I'll have a clear conscience." Although he had won ace honors, he added, "After all I suppose what you did in the war won't buy any bacon or breakfast a year from now." His prediction was not quite correct. He later became a film writer and producer whose credits include the screenplay for *The Eagle and the Hawk* (1933) about the air war.

Through those years, US president Woodrow Wilson repeatedly insisted his government behave as a true neutral by doing nothing to favor one side over the other. Nevertheless, it was clear to everyone that the United States was more sympathetic to the Allied Powers than it was to the Central Powers. The United States claimed it was willing to trade equally with all the belligerent nations, but the reality was different. The overwhelming bulk of US exports went to Great Britain and France, not to Germany and its allies. However, this imbalance was not due entirely to favoritism. As a practical matter, the Allies were easier to do business with because communications and shipping routes with them were more open.

American exports and financial loans helped keep the Allied Powers fighting. The German government did not regard the United States as truly neutral but wanted to avoid provoking Americans into the war on the Allies' side. That had been the main reason Germany briefly stopped its unrestricted submarine campaign after the United States protested its sinking of the ocean liner *Lusitania* in early 1915.

A century after the war, it may seem that America's entry on the Allies' side was inevitable from the start. However, that was not the case. Most Americans wanted nothing to

More than 350,000 African Americans served in the American Expeditionary Force in France. Because of the US Army's rigid racial segregation policies, most were allowed only noncombat support duties. Some, however, such as the members of the 367th Infantry pictured here, distinguished themselves in combat. Many fought alongside the French and received many decorations.

do with the war. They were disgusted with the long history of European conflicts and regarded the European War, as they called it, as none of their business. Americans were glad to be safely thousands of miles away from the fighting. Few could see any benefits they might reap from joining in. Moreover, while the war was having a devastating effect on the economies of Europe, it was helping many American industries boom. American factories and farms were growing richer supplying Europe with products the embattled countries desperately needed. While public sentiment generally favored the Allies, millions of Americans of German descent sympathized with Germany. Additional millions of Americans of Irish descent had strong anti-British feelings because of the long history of British domination of Ireland.

The US Declaration of War

ON NOVEMBER 7, 1916, Woodrow Wilson was re-elected president of the United States. Because he had campaigned on the slogan "He kept us out of war," his election reflected the general antiwar mood of the country. On March 4, 1917, he delivered his second inaugural address, in which he reiterated his call for America to "stand firm in armed neutrality." Less than one month later, however, he asked Congress for a declaration of war against Germany. On April 6, Congress acted on his request and the United States entered World War I.

During the months leading up to that declaration, Wilson had worked hard to persuade European leaders to meet together to negotiate a peace. More than two years of fighting had killed millions of people and devastated Europe's economies, and no end was in sight. Germany had responded positively to Wilson's overtures, but France and Britain rejected them. Both countries were uneasy about Wilson's apparent willingness to treat Germany leniently. They wanted to make Germany pay for what they had already suffered.

In January 1917, Germany announced it would resume unrestricted submarine warfare and begin sinking all ships suspected of carrying supplies to the Allies. When a U-boat sank the American cargo ship *Housatonic* on February 3, President Wilson immediately cut off diplomatic relations with Germany. That signaled a shift in his attitude toward the war. Later the same month, another event moved the United States even closer to entering the war. Great Britain revealed it had intercepted a coded telegram from German foreign minister Alfred Zimmermann to his embassy in Mexico City. The telegram ordered Germany's ambassador to urge Mexico to go to war against the United States. In return,

President Woodrow Wilson announcing to Congress he has broken diplomatic relations with Germany.

Germany would promise Mexico substantial aid to reconquer territories Mexico had lost during the 19th century. Mexico was at the time unhappy about recent US incursions, but its government was in no condition to go to war with anyone—especially not the United States.

A few days before Wilson's inauguration, he had the contents of the Zimmermann telegram published in newspapers across the United States. Although the idea of Mexico's reconquering parts of the United States was ridiculous, Americans were outraged. Public opinion swiftly shifted in favor of American entry into the Allied war against Germany. Germany's continued sinking of American ships helped harden public opinion against it.

An immediate concern for the United States after it entered the war was to deal with the problem of German submarines. In addition to wanting to protect its own and Allied ships from being sunk, it had to ensure the safety of the millions of troops it would send to Europe. To that end, it joined with Britain to develop a convoy system in the North Atlantic. All ships sailing from North America were grouped together in convoys that were escorted across the ocean by British and American naval vessels. The convoys were an immediate and dramatic success. Before the system started, one in four ships sailing to Britain was sunk. By the end of the year, sinkings had dropped to one in 25 ships.

Mobilization

AMERICA'S FIRST order of business after declaring war was to build up its armed forces. Although Germany had wanted to keep Americans out of the war, it had been confident that the United States lacked the military manpower and weapons to pose a major threat immediately. That view was largely correct. In 1917, the US Navy had a substantial fleet of modern warships but was short on manpower, with only 66,000 sailors and officers. The war would be settled primarily on the ground, and the US Army had only 127,600 men in the Regular Army troops and 80,400 National Guardsmen in federal service. The Marine Corps had only 16,000 men under arms. The German, British, and French armies had each been losing more men in single offensives than were in the entire US Army and Marine Corps.

Part of the reason the United States was so poorly prepared for war was President Wilson's strict insistence on appearing neutral. His policy kept the military from behaving like it expected to go to war. Thus, when the nation finally *did* go to war, it had a lot of catching up to do in a hurry. Congress authorized a huge expansion of military manpower,

Search for a Convoy

AFTER ALLIED NAVIES started grouping ships together in convoys to cross the Atlantic, they could provide them with much better protection against submarines. The convoy system also had another advantage. On the huge expanses of the Atlantic, submarines had almost as much trouble finding a convoy of 20 to 30 ships as they had finding a single ship. When 20 Allied ships sailed separately, a submarine had 20 chances of finding one. If the same 20 ships sailed together, the submarine had only one chance of finding them. To appreciate why this is true, you can perform a simple experiment in which you play the role of a submarine hunting for ships on the ocean.

Materials

- ✪ Brown paper grocery bag
- ✪ Paper hole puncher
- ✪ Large lawn
- ✪ Friend to serve as your assistant
- ✪ Stopwatch or other timing device
- ✪ Notepad
- ✪ Pen or pencil

In this experiment, a large lawn will represent the ocean, and small pieces of paper will represent ships. When you pretend to be a submarine, you will need to crawl on your knees, so dress appropriately. The lawn area should be at least as large as a tennis or basketball court for your experiment to work properly.

Use a hole puncher to make at least 50 pieces of chad from a brown paper bag. Do not use white or brightly colored paper; ships should be hard to see. Collect the pieces in groups of 20. Take them to a lawn where you can find enough space to perform your experiment without getting in anyone else's way. While you are not watching, have a friend randomly scatter 20 pieces of chad over the area you designate as the North Atlantic. Then, have the friend time how long it takes you to find only one "ship." Record that time on a notepad. Pocket the chad you find and repeat the experiment from the same starting point four more times.

After you have completed five searches, have your friend group 20 more pieces of chad closely together as a "convoy" somewhere on the lawn—again without your watching. Then have your friend time how long it takes you to find the convoy. Ignore the single pieces of chad already on the lawn. Collect the convoy chad, record your time, and repeat the whole experiment four more times. If you conduct your experiment correctly, the average time you take to find the "convoy" should be considerably longer than the average time required to find one "ship."

Keep in mind that if you really were a submarine, you would be searching from surface level, not from above like an airplane. It is essential you search from close to ground level. Try lying flat on the lawn and imagine looking for ships from that perspective. That would be closer to what submarines actually did.

and large-scale recruiting campaigns began. In May, President Wilson signed into law the Selective Service Act of 1917. It allowed for the eventual drafting of 2.8 million men into military service.

Meanwhile, the various military services began building scores of new training camps around the country to accommodate the rapid influx of new recruits. Complex arrangements were made to supply the new personnel with the uniforms, military gear, and other supplies they would need both in training and in combat. Some recruits were surprised by the amount of training they went through. An army lieutenant named Sam Woodfill later wrote that he had joined with "visions of being rushed to the firing line with orders to break through, push on to Berlin and capture the Kaiser. We figured they'd shoot us across on the next boat. But we guessed wrong. Instead of sending us to war they sent us to school."

The expansion occurred so rapidly that many army recruits had to train with wooden rifles until real weapons could be supplied. When army troops reached France, they were issued metal helmets made by the British because helmets were not even being manufactured in the United States.

Public Reactions

THE FEDERAL government also moved quickly to create a propaganda agency. The new Committee for Publication Information soon began waging a propaganda campaign to drum up public support for the war. The committee cranked out endless streams of posters, pamphlets, and films and built up a body of public speakers to promote the war effort. A large part of the propaganda campaign focused on selling

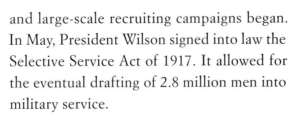

Army trainees at New Jersey's Fort Dix training center about to be shipped out to Europe.

Learn the Lyrics of the War's Most Popular Song

EVERY WAR HAS inspired memorable songs, ranging from the Civil War's joyously spirited "When Johnny Comes Marching Home" to the solemnly patriotic "Ballad of the Green Berets" of the Vietnam War. World War I also produced memorable songs. Among the best known today are "It's a Long Way to Tipperary," "Oh! How I Hate to Get Up in the Morning," and "Pack Up Your Troubles in Your Old Kit-Bag." The war's best-known song in America, however, is "Over There." George M. Cohan wrote it the same morning he learned of America's entry into the war. A rousing call to arms with unforgettably rhythmic lyrics, the song sold two million copies of sheet music before the war ended. Cohan himself was later awarded the Congressional Medal of Honor for contributions his songs made to the American spirit.

Materials

✪ Access to the Internet

You can use the lyrics printed here to memorize the song. Think about what its words mean. Who is "calling"? Who are the "sons of liberty"? Where is the "there" in "over there"? Who should "beware"? ("Hun," incidentally, was a disrespectful Allied nickname for Germans.) If you have a computer or device that gives you access to the web, go to www.YouTube.com and search for "Over There" to find recordings of the song you can listen to.

"Over There"

Johnnie, get your gun, get your gun, get your gun,
Take it on the run, on the run, on the run;
Hear them calling you and me; Ev'ry son of liberty.
Hurry right away, no delay, go today,
Make your daddy glad, to have had such a lad,

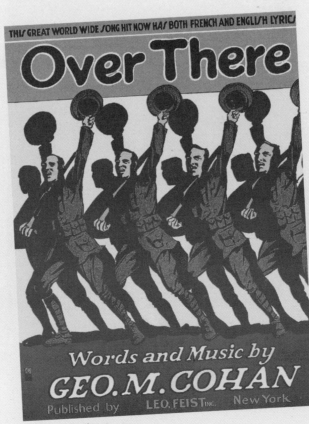

THIS GREAT WORLD WIDE SONG HIT NOW HAS BOTH FRENCH AND ENGLISH LYRICS

Over There

Words and Music by
GEO. M. COHAN

Published by LEO. FEIST INC. New York

Collection of the author

Tell your sweetheart not to pine, To be proud her boy's in line.

(chorus)
Over there, over there,
Send the word, send the word over there,
That the Yanks are coming, the Yanks are coming,
The drums rum-tumming ev'rywhere.
So prepare, say a pray'r,
Send the word, send the word to beware,
We'll be over, we're coming over,
And we won't come back till it's over over there.

(next verse)
Johnnie, get your gun, get your gun, get your gun,
Johnnie show the Hun, you're a son of a gun,
Hoist the flag and let her fly, Like true heroes do or die,
Pack your little kit, show your grit, do your bit,
Soldiers to the ranks from the towns and the tanks,
Make your mother proud of you, And to liberty be true.

(repeat chorus)

"Liberty Bonds" to finance the war. Essentially a form of loans the government would pay back later, the bonds would cover about two-thirds of the cost of the war. The campaigns were so successful they were regularly oversubscribed.

It took nearly a year for the United States to bring its military forces to full fighting strength. By the end of the war, the US Army would number 3.7 million men. More than half of them were sent to Europe. The US Navy and Marine Corps increased their own numbers almost as fast. In less than two full years, American military forces as a whole grew 15 times larger. This rapid increase put enormous strains on the country to meet the stupendous demands to organize, house, clothe, feed, equip, and train all the new soldiers, Marines, and sailors. America's ability to meet those demands was an impressive testament to both its industrial strength and its will. No other country could have achieved as much in the same length of time.

The first American army and Marine troops sent to Europe arrived in late May 1917. After landing in Britain, they were sent on to France to join the American Expeditionary Force (AEF) being organized by General John J. Pershing. US Marine troops remained in their own brigades but would fight within US Army divisions. The British and French were eager to incorporate the newly arriving American troops directly into their own armies to replace their losses, but Pershing resisted their pleas. He insisted on keeping American troops together under American command. That decision would have important consequences for establishing the identity of the American army.

By summer, American troops were landing in France in increasing numbers. Almost all of them were raw recruits when they arrived.

Film comedian Charles Chaplin speaking in support of Liberty Bonds in Washington, DC, in early 1918.

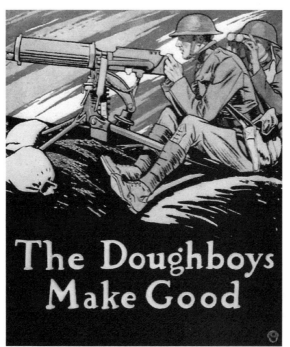

The Doughboys Make Good

Cover of *Collier's Magazine* celebrating the bravery and skill of the men in the American Expeditionary Force in France. American troops were affectionately called "doughboys" during the war. The nickname's exact origin is not known, but it went back at least as far as the Civil War.

Most knew little about Europeans and spoke only English, so misunderstandings could occur easily. A US Army officer recalled the moment his troopship landed at France: An enthusiastic "Frenchman raised his cap and waved to the soldiers leaning over the rail and cried, 'Vive l'Amerique! Vive les Americaines!' A doughboy on the deck called back through his hands, 'Vive yourself, you damned frog!'" The young American apparently did not realize that *vive*, French for "long live," was a high compliment but probably knew calling a Frenchman a "frog" was an insult.

The recruits completed their training in France with the help of French veterans of the war. Meanwhile, Germany hoped to end the

ABOVE: **Enthusiastic American troops embarking for Europe. An army recruit named Frederick A. Pottle later described his departure from his southern training camp to the North as a long, "triumphal procession" that made him "quite drunk with the excitement of it."**

BELOW: **The first American soldiers and sailors who arrived in Europe were warmly welcomed in Allied cities.**

General John J. Pershing (right) with General Douglas Haig, who commanded British army forces in France from 1915 to 1917.

war with a major offensive against the British and French on the western front before enough Americans arrived to make a difference. Technically, the United States was never a formal member of the Allies but was merely fighting its own war against Germany. It did not even declare war against Austria-Hungary until December 1917, and it never declared war against the Ottoman Empire.

The only US military service to enlist women with full military ranks and pay was the navy. By the end of the war, about 11,000 women had done administrative work as navy yeomen. Another 16,000 American women served with the American Expeditionary Force in France. Many of them had jobs as civilian employees of the military. They worked in medicine, physical and occupational therapy, relief work, administration, and other fields. The vast majority were nurses, clerical workers, canteen workers, and telephone operators. A contingent of nurses was, in fact, among the first Americans to go to France. They worked with the British Expeditionary Force before substantial numbers of American troops began arriving.

Few armies used women in combat units, but rumors of regiments of fierce "Amazon" women fighting for Germany circulated among American troops. An American army officer said that many soldiers "thought that it would be nice to capture and try to tame an Amazon. Usually we had been away from women for so long that even a woman behind a machine gun would add interest to our existence." The women Americans occasionally saw behind enemy lines were generally singers and dancers sent to the front to entertain troops, just as French, British, and American women entertained Allied troops.

Unlike the US Army, the Russian army used women in combat. After winning distinction on the eastern front, these Russian women were made instructors to inspire new recruits.

Coin a Slogan

SLOGANS ARE CATCHY phrases designed to move people to do things. Presidential campaigns have long used snappy slogans such as "We Want Wilkie" and "I Like Ike" to win votes. Advertisers use slogans as simple as "Got Milk?" and "It's the real thing" to get people to buy products. Wars also inspire slogans. They serve to rally national support, inspire citizens to take up military service, or get people to contribute to fund-raising campaigns.

Wartime slogans work best when they evoke emotional responses. During the Spanish-American War, for example, Americans were constantly told "Remember the *Maine*!" to stir their anger against Spain, which had allegedly blown up the battleship *Maine* in Cuba. During the second world war, "Remember Pearl Harbor!" kept Americans thinking about Japan's attack on Hawaii's naval base. Liberty Bond campaigns during World War I stirred Americans with "Remember Belgium," "Beat back the Hun," and other slogans designed to make them think of Germans as dangerous barbarians. The war's most popular recruiting slogan in the United States was "I want YOU for the U.S. Army," which always appeared below a painting of Uncle Sam pointing directly at readers.

Materials

✪ Writing or printing paper
✪ Pen or pencil, or computer

See if you can coin at least one entirely original slogan for World War I. Begin by deciding at whom you wish to aim your slogan. You need not restrict yourself to writing for Americans. In fact, you might find it more interesting to write a slogan for Germany (if you do that, pretend everyone speaks English, unless you happen to know German). Next, decide the purpose of your slogan. The many possibilities may include

☆ drumming up general support for the war
☆ attracting military recruits
☆ launching a scrap-metal drive
☆ persuading citizens to waste less food
☆ encouraging people to write letters to men and women serving overseas

After you select a subject, think of how it might have affected people emotionally during the war. Word your slogan to draw out those emotions. Try poetical devices, such as alliteration and rhymes, to make your wording catchy. Keep your slogan as brief as possible.

10
THE HOME FRONTS

IN ADDITION TO its unprecedented geographical extent, World War I introduced something else new to warfare by affecting civilian populations in ways never before experienced. Aerial bombing and long-range artillery brought the terrors of combat directly into civilian homes. The need to keep vast forces constantly supplied with food, equipment, arms and ammunition, airplanes, ships, and vehicles at the same time able-bodied men were being lost to military service taxed countries to their breaking points. Governments assumed ever greater control over every aspect of peoples' lives.

As the war ground on, it affected more and more aspects of the daily lives of civilians. Accustomed freedoms were taken away, shortages of all kinds of consumer goods made life harder, traveling became more difficult, and life in general became harsher and less comfortable. At the same time, people grew more anxious about how the war was going, and more and more families lost sons, brothers, and fathers in the fighting.

Throughout the war, civilians at home did not forget the men at arms. Most families in the European nations had close family members fighting in the war. To cheer them up and assure the men they were remembered, relatives wrote them many letters and sent them parcels with sweets, tobacco, books, and other things. Troops serving in the trenches particularly welcomed wool socks to keep their feet warm. In Britain, knitting socks and other garments for soldiers became a national fad. Men, women, and children could be seen knitting almost everywhere.

What was happening at home became as important to the war as what was happening on battlefronts. Indeed, it was said that behind every man serving at a battlefront stood at least three civilian workers who maintained him. A new term that emerged during the war was "home front." It is a very appropriate description of the civilian side of the war.

Despite the general hardening of conditions and miseries that people suffered, the war brought positive changes. In most of the countries, it helped break down social class distinctions. Even more significantly, it advanced the emancipation of women by bringing them into the workplace, thereby widening their future economic opportunities. It also helped them win the right to vote in several countries after long years of struggling for political equality. In Great Britain, for example, the Representation of the People Act of 1918 lowered the voting age for men to 18 to reward young soldiers returning from the war. For their contributions to the war effort, women were also granted some voting rights. Full voting equality would not come until 1928, but the 1918 law was a huge turning point.

Recruiting

THE OUTBREAK of war was generally greeted with enthusiasm on the home fronts of the first countries involved. Patriotic excitement made recruiting soldiers and sailors comparatively easy at first, especially as almost everyone expected the war to end quickly. In Britain, all that was initially required was a recruitment campaign based on the slogan "Your King and Country Need *You!*" Thousands of young men eagerly rushed to sign up. Throughout the first year of the war, recruiting posters were everywhere.

However, as the war wore on and proved to be incredibly brutal, recruiting men to fight grew increasingly difficult. Faced with the prospect of not having enough manpower to

Write a Letter from Home to a Soldier in Europe

SOLDIERS AND SAILORS serving in the war craved news from home so much that mail calls were often the highlights of their day. One British soldier called receiving letters from family "one of the best pleasures of life," even better than "not being thirsty, nor hungry, nor cold, nor afraid." However, the friends, relatives, and sweethearts writing to them needed to be careful about what they said so as not to add to the miseries service personnel were already suffering. Soldiers uncertain they would live through the war did not need to hear things were going badly at home when they could do nothing to help.

To appreciate the challenge of writing an honest but morale-lifting letter to a serviceman, imagine yourself living during World War I with someone you care about very much serving in the war. Write that person a letter.

Materials

- ✪ Stationery paper
- ✪ Note paper
- ✪ Ink pen

To write as most people did during the early 20th century, use a pen, not a computer, and use good stationery paper. Try to write as neatly as possible to make a good impression on the recipient. Before you begin to write, jot down notes on exactly who you are: Are you American, Canadian, British, French, German, or another nationality? Do you live in a city or in the country? Are you the child, sibling, friend, or sweetheart of the person to whom you are writing? The answers to these and other questions will affect what you say in your letter.

Bonne Année

Crois aux souhaits de mon amour Filial
Ainsi que je crois au succès Final .

DIX
405,4

Write notes on the kinds of news you might pass along, such as recent births and deaths in your family, what has been happening around your home, how the family pets are doing, how favorite sports teams are faring, and what neighbors and friends are up to.

After jotting down all the ideas you can think of, use them to compose your letter in a way likely to cheer up its recipient. If you wish to comment on how the war is affecting your community, remember that people serving in a war zone would not want to hear that things are worse at home than where they are. At the same time, do not make up good things that have not really happened. Your recipient would either not believe them or later be disappointed to discover they were not true.

The printed message on this French postcard is apparently addressed to the boy's father fighting at the front. The boy wishes him a happy new year and asks him to believe in his love as much as he himself believes in ultimate success in the war.

Collection of the author

win the war, governments turned to mandatory conscription. France and Germany already had conscription, but the idea was alien to Britain, where it violated cherished principles of personal liberty. By mid-1915, however, it was becoming apparent that voluntary enlistments would not meet Britain's military manpower needs. Britain's Parliament enacted a mandatory draft registration law, and pressures on civilian men to enlist voluntarily grew stronger. Men of military age who hesitated to sign up were often derided as unpatriotic cowards and shamed into enlisting.

By January 1916, it was clear that Britain could not reach its manpower needs merely through voluntary enlistments. For the first time in British history, the government imposed mandatory conscription. As the government drafted increasing numbers of men into military service, shortages of men in important industries became a problem.

Conscription was also used to build up the US Army. Before the United States entered World War I, it had had a tradition of all-volunteer military service in wars. The one exception had been the Civil War, in which both the Union and the Confederacy tried conscription to raise troops. That experience had been a bad one because of the gross unfairness with which conscription was used. There was enough opposition to the world war in the country to have reason to fear a repetition of the draft riots of the Civil War, but that did not happen. The government went straight to mobilizing for conscription as soon as the country entered the war. After registering 23.9 million men, the Selective Service system eventually drafted 2.8 million of them. Another two million men volunteered for service. Most of the volunteers went into the navy.

Censorship of News

DURING THE early 20th century, television and the Internet did not exist yet, and radio broadcasting was still in its experimental stages. People in countries fighting in the war got most of their information about the war from newspapers. What they read was not always truthful or complete. Government press censorship was common. It was justified by the need to suppress information that might be useful to enemies. All countries in the war experienced at least some press censorship.

In France, the military severely limited what was published in the press. What the public read was not necessarily untrue, but it was incomplete. Censorship extended to soldiers, who were not allowed to mention any military subjects in their letters. The British government also tightly controlled the press, but through a civilian bureau, not the military.

In Germany, censorship went further. There the military controlled the press. It dictated what papers should say about the war, which the press was told to blame on Britain. As the war progressed, the German public got an increasingly distorted view of what was really happening. This had a profound effect on the country when the war ended. For four years, the German people were repeatedly told their country was an innocent victim of foreign aggression but was nevertheless winning the war. When the war ended with Germany's sudden surrender and its subsequent acceptance of responsibility for starting the war, Germans were shocked and felt betrayed.

In the growing absence of reliable public news sources in countries fighting the war, unfounded rumors spread rapidly. Some false rumors told people what they wanted to hear— that their wartime enemies were starting to surrender and that their own troops were scoring major victories. Other rumors spread more frightening stories about enemies at their doorsteps. When the war began, all the countries involved had many residents who were citizens of their new enemies' countries: British teachers in Germany, German governesses in Britain, and countless others. These people suddenly found themselves unwelcome aliens. Some managed to get out quickly and return to their own countries. Others were left at the mercy of unfriendly governments and populations. Germany, for example, imprisoned and interned a large number of British nationals, and the British government interned many Germans. Fear of spies and saboteurs was widespread. Even the Canadian and Australian governments interned resident Germans.

An unfortunate aspect of public reactions to the war in the United States was a turning against German Americans. Many German immigrants were persecuted. Some Americans even advocated banning the German language in the United States. Some towns with obviously German names, such as Berlin, adopted new names, such as Liberty. Some people even started calling the sauerkraut on their hot dogs "liberty cabbage."

As is typical during wars, rumors, however absurd, spread rapidly, raising public uneasiness. In Britain, German governesses were believed to have bombs hidden in their trunks. As the war progressed and hatred toward enemy nations grew, members of the public often turned on local foreign nationals and wrecked their homes and places of business. Real enemy actions, such as Germany's sinking of the passenger liner *Lusitania* and the bombing of civilian homes, added to those ill feelings.

Like its European allies, the United States also instituted government censorship of news. Shortly after the country entered the war, Congress started passing a series of strict laws empowering the government to censor speech and the press. At the same time, it initiated propaganda programs to promote patriotism. In late 1917, the executive branch of the government created the Censorship Board. The federal government used its power over the US Post Office to limit what newspapers and magazines could be mailed.

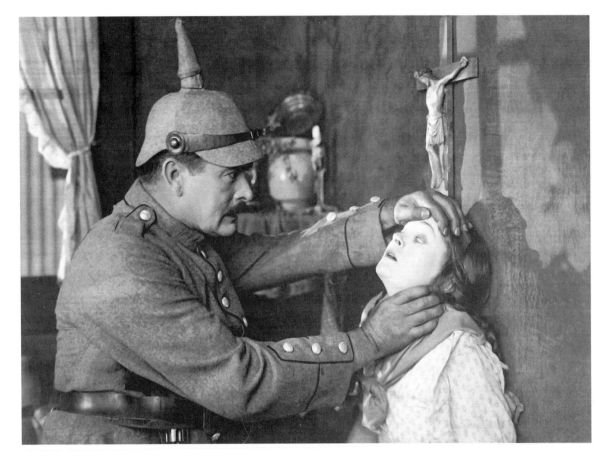

The Propaganda War

THE OTHER side of government suppression of information through censorship is propaganda. Propaganda is the dissemination of information that may or may not be true to promote a particular point of view. It is designed to win support for the government's cause, while discrediting the enemy's cause. Propaganda can take many forms—from repeatedly calling attention to real successes to spreading outright lies.

One of the most extreme forms propaganda took during the war was the invention of stories about enemy atrocities—lies about the terrible things enemies did. For example, Allied propaganda told horrifying stories about German soldiers senselessly mutilating and killing innocent women and even spearing babies with their bayonets. German propaganda told similarly awful stories about the Allies. The effect of such propaganda was to intensify hatred for the enemy and thereby build support for each nation's war effort.

Americans were subject to wartime propaganda long before the United States entered the war. The day after Great Britain declared

Scene from the 1918 propaganda film *Stake Uncle Sam to Play Your Hand*, which was designed to raise American anger against Germany.

war on Germany, it cut the telegraph cables connecting Germany to the United States. From that date, Americans got most of their news of the war from Britain. British propaganda organizations worked hard to spread their view of the war to the United States and other countries. The British message was that Germany was evil. Meanwhile, German propaganda agencies were also at work in the United States. Much of the material they distributed offered reasoned defenses of Germany's actions in the war, while also calling attention to alleged atrocities of the Allies.

Bringing the War Home

DESPITE THE vast extent and ferocity of World War I, the war did not inflict nearly as much destruction on western Europe's civilian populations as the next world war would two decades later. The farmlands of northern France and Belgium were devastated, but few major cities suffered extensive damage. German cities were almost untouched by combat. During the last year of the war, Paris was bombarded by long-range artillery but suffered only minor damage. The British were shocked by German bombing attacks and a few naval bombardments of coastal towns, but their cities also suffered only minor damage. Nevertheless, fear of bombing attacks had a powerful psychological effect.

War Material Industries

THE WAR affected the manufacturing industries of each nation involved differently. Germany had the most fully developed war materials industries at the start of the war but had to get through the war without outside help. Its advanced chemical and electrical industries depended on imported raw materials it could not easily get because of the Allied blockade. Its supply of petroleum from the United States, for example, was cut off. It was also running out of rubber needed for vehicle tires, electrical engine parts, and other products. To compensate for such shortages, the government restricted nonmilitary uses of many raw materials, while chemists and engineers looked for substitutes. Eventually, the Germans learned how to make synthetic rubber and how to convert their abundant coal supplies to petroleum. Meanwhile, the Germans converted many plants that had been making consumer products to munitions factories. A large piano factory, for example, switched to making artillery shells.

By late 1915, Germany was running short on metals used in munitions. The government called for inventories of all copper and brass in households. Soon, people were selling pots and pans, candlesticks, door knobs, light fixtures, and all manner of household goods to the government to be melted down for military uses. By the end of the war, Germans were melting down church bells to make artillery shells and were tearing lead pipes up from streets.

Britain lacked the advanced chemical and engineering industries that Germany already had. Unlike Germany, however, it had direct access to world markets for the raw products it needed. Its conversion to large-scale wartime production was therefore very different. France's prewar industrial condition was similar to that of Britain. It was, however, handicapped by Germany's occupation of much of its most important industrial region in the northeast.

One of the first crises in Allied war production was a critical shortage of artillery shells in Britain. Artillery guns were firing explosive shells faster than British factories could make them. Inadequate shell supplies threatened British troops on the western front with being outgunned. While both Germany and France were manufacturing hundreds of thousands of artillery shells every day, Britain was only making hundreds. That shortage became a political scandal in 1915 that led to a change in the government. David Lloyd George was made minister of munitions. Under his leadership, the government instituted plans to compel industries to increase munitions production. By the following year, munitions factories were turning out bullets, shells, and explosives at rates as much as 15 times greater than in the first two years of the war. Lloyd George's success in that endeavor would later help make him prime minister through the last few years of the war.

Women Around the World

ALTHOUGH WOMEN were not allowed to serve in the military forces of most of the nations fighting, they nevertheless made vital contributions to the war. Most countries created auxiliary military services for women. These services performed mostly noncombatant duties that had been performed by men in the regular military services—secretaries and administrative work, telegraphists and code workers, electricians, and other jobs. Britain created the WRNS, or "Wrens" (Women's Royal Naval Service); WAAC (Women's Auxiliary Army Corps), and WRAF (Women's Royal Air Force). The United States did not at that time have similar services for American women, but many women in the United States made valuable contributions to the war effort as civilian workers.

As military forces drained men from each country, many women moved into jobs they had never held before to take their places.

Before the war, it was unusual for middle-class women to work outside their homes. By introducing millions of these women to the workplace, the war helped free women from restrictions on what they were allowed to do. In Britain, many women who had been employed previously were domestic servants, who worked outside their homes out of economic necessity. Hundreds of thousands of them took up better-paying war-related jobs and never returned to domestic service.

Without women workers, the munitions industries that kept Britain's armies and navies fighting would have collapsed. Women helped build tanks, airplanes, guns, bullets, artillery shells, and bombs. They also took up agricultural work to keep farms producing and moved into other kinds of jobs left behind by men.

As France lost increasing numbers of men to the war, the government strongly promoted the employment of women in jobs previously held by men to free up men for the military. In 1916, it passed a law making it illegal to hire a man to do any job that could be done by a woman. Eventually, women far outnumbered men in arms factories.

In Britain, women were eager to help in the war effort. After the government created the Ministry of Munitions, women entered munitions factories in large numbers. As early as the end of 1915, female workers in munitions

Poster encouraging American women to support a fund-raising campaign for the war.

How Much Sugar Is in Your Food?

WHEN WE READ about people having less sugar during the war, our thoughts are likely to go to tasty dessert items—candies, cookies, cakes, pies, and other sweet treats. Such foods naturally have high sugar contents and could not easily be made without sugar. However, sugar is used in many foods that we may not think of as being sweet. For example, it is an important ingredient in many bread products.

To gain an understanding of what the loss of sugar meant to the countries fighting in World War I, make an inventory of the amounts of sugar in packaged foods in your home. People living a century ago did not have the same processed foods we eat today, but studying how sugar fits into the ingredients of modern packaged foods will give you some appreciation of what it would mean not to have sugar in your diet.

Materials

- Lined notepad or paper
- Pencil or pen
- Calculator (optional)

Study the ingredient and "nutrition facts" labels of packaged foods in your home's pantry and refrigerator. Write down the name of each product, its recommended serving size (usually given in grams), and the number of grams of sugar in a single serving. Divide the number of grams of sugar by the grams in a serving to calculate what percentage of the product is sugar. For example, if there are 5 grams of sugar in a 25-gram serving, sugar constitutes 20 percent of the product by weight.

Examine as many different foods as you can find—breads, breakfast cereals, canned fruits and vegetables, sauces, and frozen products. You will probably be surprised by the amount of sugar in what we eat.

plants outnumbered male workers three to one. Their liberation was far from complete, however, as they generally received only a fraction of the wages men received. Nevertheless, women workers in Britain and France earned enough money to enjoy a financial independence they had not previously known.

An unpleasant reality of the war that deserves more attention is the suffering many women endured while working in factories. Even seemingly harmless jobs like painting airplanes were dangerous. The fumes given off by varnish used on airplane wings were so toxic that a large percentage of the painters were often too sick to work. The chemicals used in munitions factories were even more dangerous, giving workers symptoms like those of pneumonia and jaundice and turning their skin yellow. Many women worked hard 12 hours a day and also spent many hours commuting. Accidents were a problem, too. In early 1917, an explosion in an East London munitions factory caused more than 450 casualties, most of whom were women.

Food

THE COMMODITY of greatest importance to both military and civilian populations was, of course, food. Everyone must eat. Even with its rising death tolls, the war did not significantly reduce the numbers of mouths that had to be fed. It did, however, significantly reduce the numbers of hands available to produce food. The millions of male farm workers off fighting in war stopped contributing to food production but continued to eat. Their places in the agricultural fields were partly filled by women and children. In 1916 alone, Britain put out a call to recruit 400,000 women farm workers.

The war also disrupted international trade patterns that had helped keep nations fed. Before the war, Germany had consumed more food than it produced itself. The Allied blockade on Germany's trade forced it to increase its own food production to make up for its reduced imports. This was not easy, however, because its own agriculture also relied on imported materials, especially chemical fertilizers. The country also was running out of agricultural workers.

In January 1915, only five months after the war began, Germany introduced bread rationing. As the war went on, it rationed other food items, and the amounts people could buy were steadily reduced. To make up for shortages, Germans substituted inferior items for their regular foods. This practice gave the world the German word *ersatz* for inferior substitutes. Examples include roasted acorns and beechnuts for coffee beans, ground berry leaves for tea, and ashes mixed with pepper. Substitute

goods also extended into other products, notably clothing. Cotton almost disappeared and other fabrics were becoming rare, too, so substitutes were found.

The result of Germany's food problems should be obvious. Malnutrition became a growing problem, and by the end of the war,

After entering the war, the United States joined Europe in campaigning against wasting foods, especially meats and wheat.

National Archives and Records Administration

Bake War Bread

TO MAKE UP for war-caused shortages in common foodstuffs such as sugar and wheat flour, Americans were encouraged to adapt recipes using substitute items. This recipe for "war bread" uses no sugar or lard, which were standard ingredients in bread before the war.

Adult supervision required

Ingredients
- 1 cup hot tap water
- ½ tablespoon shortening
- 1 teaspoon corn syrup
- 2¼ teaspoons active dry yeast (about one standard packet)
- 1 teaspoon salt
- 3 cups bread flour

Utensils
- Measuring cup
- Mixing spoon
- Mixing bowl
- Flour sifter
- Breadboard
- Clean cloth
- 8½ × 4½ × 2½-in. baking pan
- Oven
- Cooling rack
- Bread knife

Allow about two hours and 45 minutes to prepare and bake this bread. Mix the hot water, shortening, and corn syrup in a large bowl until the corn syrup is completely dissolved. After the mixture cools to a lukewarm temperature, mix in the dry yeast and salt. Gradually add the flour, using a sifter, until the mixture is doughy enough to knead by hand. With freshly washed hands, knead the dough on a lightly floured breadboard for about eight minutes. Use the flour sifter to dust the dough lightly as you knead it.

Use a small amount of shortening to grease the mixing bowl and the dough. Place the dough in the bowl and cover it with a damp cloth. Set the bowl in a warm place. After an hour, the dough should double in size. Use your clean fist to punch it down and then turn it out onto a floured breadboard. Knead it again for five minutes.

Form the dough into one loaf and place it in a greased bread pan. Cover it with the cloth and let it rise until it again doubles in size, in about 30 minutes. After 15 minutes, set your oven to 375 degrees Fahrenheit with the supervision of an adult. When the dough has risen, put the pan in the oven and let the bread bake for 45 minutes or until its top is golden brown. When it is done, turn it onto a rack to cool. After it has cooled, cut slices with a bread knife.

Eat the bread without butter or margarine, which you probably would not have had during the war.

many Germans were literally starving to death. Troops at the front were also feeling the effects of food shortages, even though keeping them fed was a government priority.

The war increased food prices in Britain, but that country did not face serious shortages for some time. Toward the end of 1916, however, the government started encouraging people to grow their own food in whatever unused plots of lands they could find. By the following year, vegetables were seen sprouting almost everywhere—in backyards, empty lots, corners of public parks and golf courses, and dozens of other places. Germans adopted the same practice and started growing potatoes and other vegetables everywhere they could.

Although Britain was in a stronger position than Germany for feeding itself, it too eventually faced a food crisis. Germany's goal was to starve Britain by sinking most of the ships carrying food and supplies to it. In 1917, Germany's unrestricted submarine campaign finally was starting to hurt Britain seriously. The supply of imported sugar and wheat was hit particularly hard. The government resisted the idea of ordering mandatory rationing and instead campaigned to get people voluntarily to consume less of some foods, to substitute certain foods, and to waste less food. At the same time, it looked for ways to increase agricultural production.

France was finally feeling the effects of food shortages, too. As in Britain, sugar and wheat were in particularly short supply. Long accustomed to serving generous amounts of bread with their meals, the French were forced to accept inferior substitutes and change their eating habits.

Opposition to the War

CIVILIAN POPULATIONS generally supported their governments' involvement in the war, even as conditions worsened. Serious opposition to the war did, however, emerge in some countries. In Britain, for example, a number of antiwar and anticonscription movements arose.

Britain's No-Conscription Fellowship held the principle that

no state in the world has any right . . . to tamper with the unfettered free right of every man to decide for himself the issue of life or death. We contend that the individual conscience alone must decide whether a man will sacrifice his own life, or inflict death upon other people.

The United States had its own strong antiwar movement. Many opponents of the war who were of draft age claimed conscientious objector status. Many of them were taken into noncombat service, such as medical corps.

11

ENDING THE FIGHTING

A FTER MORE THAN two years of exhausting fighting that gave neither side a significant advantage, the war finally approached its turning point in 1917. The collapse of Russia's monarchy early that year gave Germany hope that Russia would drop out of the war. When that happened, Germany would be able to move nearly one million troops from the east to the western front. America's entry into the war in April increased Germany's desire for Russia to quit fighting. Germany's strategy in 1917 was to close down its eastern front and then end the war in the west before American forces could make a difference. It did not expect the Americans to be ready to fight quickly. Meanwhile, German submarines continued to sink Allied ships as fast as they could as part of Germany's strategy to starve the Allies into submission.

Russia did drop out of the war as Germany hoped, and the Americans were as slow to get involved in fighting as it expected. Nevertheless, Germany failed to defeat France and Great Britain in 1917. By early 1918, Germany itself was in a desperate situation: by that point, its leaders knew that if they did not win the war quickly, they stood no chance of winning. So, for the first time since the opening of the war, Germany switched from a primarily defensive strategy to an offensive one. Even so, the war would drag on through most of the year.

Russia Bows Out

RUSSIA'S ENTRY into the war had been a disaster for it almost from the start. During the early months, its army had won some battles against Austria-Hungary. Afterward, however, Russia experienced mostly defeats. Much of its equipment was antiquated, and its troops were poorly trained and badly led. Its greatest advantage when it entered the war was its immense size. Its population was greater than that of all the Central Powers nations combined.

Tsar Nicholas II with his wife, Alexandra, and children in 1914. After Nicholas abdicated, he and his family were arrested and taken to Siberia. In July 1918, the entire family was executed by Bolsheviks.

No matter how badly things went, Russia was unlikely to run out of troops.

Russia's leadership problems started at the top. Tsar Nicholas II exercised even more power than Germany's Kaiser Wilhelm II. In August 1915, when the war had taken a bad turn, Nicholas assumed supreme command of his armed forces. Russia had a parliamentary body called the Duma, a prime minister, and a council of advisers. Nevertheless, no one had any real power to question the tsar's decisions. Those decisions were often poor. Under his incompetent leadership, Russia's military situation grew even worse. By 1917, about 1.5 million Russian soldiers and more than 2 million civilians had died in the war. Russia had lost immense territories to the Central Powers. The entire country was sinking under the strain of the war. Like other European countries fighting in the war, Russia was slowly starving. Food riots were becoming common, and antiwar organizations were forming everywhere.

Nicholas had never been popular, and now his reputation was worse than ever. In March, huge antigovernment demonstrations rocked Russia's capital, Petrograd (now St. Petersburg). On March 15, when Nicholas realized that neither the military nor the parliament supported him, he abdicated his throne. Russians would later remember the event as the "February Revolution" because it occurred in that month in their old-style calendar. Russia's communist revolution would come later.

With the tsar gone, a provisional socialist government was formed under Alexander Kerensky. Many Russians wanted an even more radical change, however. Peasants and workers in the major cities organized committees called "soviets" to push for land reform and Russia's withdrawal from the war. Kerensky warned, "Do not trust the promises of the Bolsheviks! Their promise of an immediate peace is a lie! Their promise to provide bread is a fraud! Their promise to distribute the land is a fairy tale for children!"

Meanwhile, although the country was falling into disorder, its new government continued to support the war. It even launched a major new offensive in July. That effort started promisingly but collapsed after Germany brought in more troops from the western front. Afterward, the Russian army began falling apart.

Politically, the country was divided into three major factions. Each held a different view about the war. Kerensky's government wanted to keep fighting until Germany and Austria-Hungary were defeated. A strong soviet faction wanted Russia to get out as soon as it could without costly territorial losses or having to pay heavy reparations. The third faction was made up of Bolsheviks, the most radical advocates of communism. They wanted

Russia out of the war immediately, regardless of the cost.

The issue was settled in early November, when the Bolsheviks, led by Vladimir Ilich Lenin, took control of the government. A few days later, Lenin announced that Russia was no longer at war. Later in the month, the Bolsheviks called for all sides in the war to stop fighting and sign a general armistice. Britain and France ignored the suggestion. In mid-December, Russia arranged a cease-fire with the Central Powers on the eastern front. A formal peace treaty would take longer. By the time it was signed in early March 1918, the former Russian Empire had lost Belarus, Bessarabia, Estonia, Finland, Latvia, Lithuania, Poland, the Ukraine, and the Caucasus region.

Russia's exit from the war freed Germany from fighting on the eastern front, letting it move 900,000 troops to the west. Germany also captured huge amounts of Russian equipment it could use against the western Allies. Under these changed conditions, the Allies' only hope for victory was that American troops would be ready for major combat before Germany could turn its strengthened forces against them.

The Western Front

ONE MIGHT think Russia's withdrawal hastened the war's end, but the opposite may have

Vladimir Ilich Lenin.

been true. By 1917, Germany was badly worn down on the western front. Without its reinforcements from the east, the Allies might have won the war sooner. Instead, as spring opened in 1918, German troops on the western front outnumbered those of the Allies for the first time since early in the war. With fresh American troops arriving in France at a rate of about 10,000 per day, Germany had to act quickly to keep its numerical advantage.

By this time, General Erich von Ludendorff was the effective ruler of Germany. Under his direction, Germany put most of its remaining strength into another giant offensive. It began north of the Somme River on March 21. Within a few days, the Germans were advancing rapidly across the Somme. It looked as though the stalemate might be broken. At the same time, Germany moved its new long-range cannons forward and used them to fire explosive artillery shells at Paris from more than 60 miles away. Hundreds of Parisians died without even knowing where the explosions were coming from.

After two weeks, the German advance stalled. Both sides were exhausted, and a new stalemate developed. Despite early successes during their offensive, the German troops were losing their morale. Worn out by years of unproductive fighting, they were running dangerously low on food and supplies. As the

British and French had retreated, the Germans had advanced so rapidly that their supplies could not keep up with them. They did not have enough horses to pull wagons. Their troops could not keep fighting without food and ammunition.

German troops were also discovering what their leaders had told them about the war was not completely true. They had been led to believe that the Allied armies were on the edge of starvation and would soon collapse. However, when they reached abandoned Allied military positions and French towns, they found stockpiles of food and supplies that were lavish in comparison to what they had been surviving on. A German soldier described what his unit found in one abandoned British position: "Tables in the kitchen are still covered with meat, cauliflower and other vegetables. The dugouts are full of provisions, and we help ourselves to cigarettes, chocolate, corned beef, condensed milk, sugar, biscuits, marmalade and other good things to eat." Such discoveries upset German soldiers' faith in their country winning the war.

Americans in Combat

AS THE German offensive slowed down, Allied leaders agreed it was time for a unified military command. In April, they made French general

Think Like a Wartime Censor

MILITARY PERSONNEL SERVING away from home need to stay in touch with their families and loved ones to keep up their morale. However, in wartime military commanders must limit what soldiers and sailors say in letters they send home. Even casual remarks in letters could be useful to enemies if they fell into the wrong hands by accident. According to one American officer who censored his troop's letters, "After the censor had finished clipping out all unauthorized information, the letters looked as though a child armed with a pair of scissors had been amusing itself by cutting paper dolls out of them."

Imagine yourself as a British army officer on the western front in 1918. One of your regular duties is to read letters the men under your command write and strike out anything that should not be said.

Materials

✪ Plain writing paper
✪ Pencil or pen
✪ Heavy black marker

The following is an imaginary letter from a British army private named Edward to his parents in England. Copy it by hand to a sheet of paper. Then read the handwritten copy carefully and look for anything that could be useful to a spy who sees it or overhears Edward's parents talking

about it. Use a heavy marker to blot out improper sentences. The result will be a letter that looks much like many real letters families received from servicemen.

April 8, 1918
Somewhere in northern France

Dear Mum and Dad,

I'm sorry I haven't written for a while. The Huns have kept us hopping. A few weeks ago, just as the weather was getting better, they started pounding our lines with artillery shells. My company was lucky. We didn't take a single hit. But the noise was deafening! The sarge said the Huns must've fired more than a million shells. I believe it.

Afterwards, the Huns came at us hard and fast. We were lucky to hold them off. I think our barbed wire saved our trench. It wasn't fun stringing that nasty stuff, but now I'm glad I helped do it. The wire saved our necks, but other companies up and down the line weren't so lucky. The next day, the generals ordered a retreat. We've pretty much kept retreating ever since. That's why I don't know exactly where we are right now. I don't think our officers know either. I'm not sure

they know much of anything. A lot of the men have been grumbling about them lately.

One of the lousy things about retreating is that we've been leaving behind supplies and equipment because we don't have any lorries or even any horses to pull wagons. This worries me because we hear the army is running short on almost everything. I don't mind eating a bit less for a while, but I don't want to run out of ammunition. We're already low on it.

I hope this letter reaches you. Don't try to send me any more food or tobacco until things settle down again. Packages may not reach me. Besides, we hear that German subs have been sinking a lot of our supply ships. Things seem grim, but we're keeping our chins up. Try not to worry about me. Remember—I'm lucky!

I hope everything at home is okay. Give everyone my love.

Your son,
Edward

THE INFLUENZA PANDEMIC

While the war was still raging in early 1918, a disaster far worse was beginning. Without any warning, a devastating influenza (flu) epidemic began sweeping the globe. Exactly how it started is not known. After spreading through almost every populated region on earth, it petered out in 1919, just as suddenly and mysteriously as it had started. Before it ended, it infected nearly half a billion people. More than 50 million people died—at least double the number killed by World War I itself. Although the flu pandemic was one of the worst disasters in human history, it is almost forgotten today.

The war did not start the flu pandemic, but it did help spread it and make it even worse. At the same time, the pandemic increased the human suffering caused by the war. The first war zone the pandemic reached was the Middle East. From there it moved north and west into Europe. Many soldiers on both sides of the war were stricken. However, because the flu hit Central Powers armies first, it gave the Allies an edge that contributed to their eventual victory. The pandemic also swept through North America, where it killed at least 500,000 people.

Ferdinand Foch commander in chief over all Allied ground forces. Meanwhile, French and British leaders were losing patience with the United States' long delay in entering the fight. General Pershing still insisted on keeping American divisions under American command and completing their training. US Army leaders did not expect most of their troops to be

American soldiers taking a musical break from the war in a wrecked church in the Argonne in October 1918.

National Archives and Records Administration

fully ready to fight until late spring in 1919. In May 1918, however, Pershing agreed to allow several hundred thousand American troops to fight with the Allied armies. As things would turn out, most of the American troops who reached France would never see any combat. Some troops who reached France were not even allowed to go ashore. Their ships simply turned around and sailed home. Americans did, however, fight in several battles toward the end of May. On May 28, they scored their first success when they liberated the town of Cantigny from German occupation and held it against fierce German counterattacks.

American reinforcements helped the Allies fend off renewed German offensives through June and July. An Allied counteroffensive combining French, British, American, and Italian troops in June killed more than 30,000 Germans. As Germany had no more reserves on which to draw, this setback was devastating. By then, German forces were falling back everywhere. Germany's unrestricted submarine warfare policy was failing, too. By the fall, everyone knew it was only a matter of time until Germany would lose the war.

Eastern Sectors of the War

ALTHOUGH THE western front remained the most important sector of the war, fighting continued in the east. Romania, which had joined the Allies in 1916, had lost most of its army by early 1918. In May, it signed a peace treaty with the Central Powers. That development made it easier for the Central Powers to push into eastern regions over which Russia's new Bolshevik government had little control. German troops advanced through the Ukraine and southern Russia, into the Caucasus region between the Caspian and Black Seas. These territories gave the Central Powers access to valuable agricultural products and petroleum.

Meanwhile, the Ottoman Empire was on the verge of collapse. After its early successes against the British at Gallipoli and in Mesopotamia, it had suffered mostly defeats. By the end of 1917, the British had occupied most of Mesopotamia and Arab revolts had driven the Turks out of Saudi Arabia. British forces under General Edmund Allenby captured Jerusalem in December. They then began advancing north to take on Turkey itself. After steadily losing ground to the British advance throughout 1918, Turkey asked for a truce in October.

The End, at Last!

THE LAST great German offensive in northern France came in July. This time, American troops played a big part in turning it back in the Second Battle of the Marne. Their stout re-sistance did not allow a single German to cross the river and forced the Germans to withdraw. Shortly afterward, General Foch launched an Allied counteroffensive while the Germans were moving their troops farther north to take on British positions. American divisions led the main attack and decisively defeated every German division they encountered.

Despite the recent influx of German troops from the eastern front, the Germans were running out of reserves to replace their losses. At the same time, fresh American troops were still pouring in. By the end of August, the Germans were on the run. The stalemate on the western front was finally broken. As fighting continued into November, the Allies steadily retook French and Belgian territories long held by the Germans. The American role in the fighting grew increasingly important.

While American troops were helping defeat the Germans through the summer of 1918, mounting troubles within Germany and Austria-Hungary were ensuring the Central Powers' doom. Citizens of both countries were fed up with the war and their political leaders. Both Germany's army and its navy experienced mutinies throughout the fall. German sailors had grown tired of having nothing to do as their great warships were confined to their ports by the British blockade. Conditions were also growing worse because the ships were not

General Edmund Allenby leading British troops into Jerusalem.

Library of Congress LC-DIG-matpc-00168

SERGEANT YORK

The most famous American hero of World War I was Alvin C. York from rural Tennessee. Because his religion opposed war, he asked to be exempted from military service when he was drafted. After being turned down, he became a reluctant private in the US Army. It happened, however, that years of shooting wild turkeys had made him an expert rifle shot. When his commanding officers in France realized how valuable that skill made him, they convinced him of the justice of fighting against the Germans. His change of attitude later served him well. It helped that he served with men whom he later called "a gang of the toughest and most hard-boiled doughboys I ever heard tell of."

In October 1918, York was on a patrol that got cut off from other troops and trapped under heavy German machine gun fire in northern France's Argonne Forest. As his comrades were being killed by streams of bullets, he found himself alone on a hill. Sitting in mud, he calmly picked off the machine gunners with his rifle. When a half-dozen Germans charged him, he shot them all. After he had killed about 20 Germans, a German officer offered to surrender all his men if York would stop killing them. With the help of seven surviving members of his patrol, York took 132 German soldiers prisoner. Afterward, he was promoted from private first class to sergeant and awarded the Congressional Medal of Honor and the French Croix de Guerre. He later returned home to find himself the most celebrated American hero of the war. Actor Gary Cooper later won an Academy Award for his portrayal of York in the 1941 film *Sergeant York*. York himself would live until 1964.

Alvin York.

being adequately supplied. The last straw came when the navy was ordered to put out to sea at the end of October in what would have been a futile attempt at winning one last blaze of glory. The sailors simply refused to go.

By then, Kaiser Wilhelm's reputation inside and outside Germany had declined so much that his ability to rule was gone. His top generals, Erich Ludendorff and Paul von Hindenburg, persuaded him to hand over his power to a new parliament. Wilhelm's cousin Prince Max von Baden was made the new chancellor. As the effective political head of the government, Prince Max began discussing peace terms with the Allies. However, with the possibility of military victory now in sight, the Allies were willing to keep fighting until Germany surrendered on their terms.

Despite the hopelessness of the situation, the Germans continued to fight hard into November. Meanwhile, Prince Max attempted to negotiate a peace settlement with US president Woodrow Wilson, bypassing France's and Britain's leaders. Earlier in the year, Wilson had indicated his willingness to treat Germany gently if it surrendered. Now, however, after Americans were being killed in the war, his attitude hardened. In early October 1918, Germany and Austria-Hungary appealed to Wilson to arrange for an armistice that would end the war without imposing penalties on either side. He replied that there could be no discussion of an armistice until all Central Powers forces were out of Belgium, France, and Serbia. Germany announced it would accept those terms, but fighting continued. While Allied leaders discussed what terms to demand from Germany, Austria-Hungary arranged its own armistice and withdrew from the war in late October.

One of the Allied conditions was the end of military dictatorship in Germany. When General Ludendorff resigned his position on October 26, that condition was met. What the Allies really wanted, however, was for Kaiser Wilhelm to abdicate. Wilhelm wanted to stay in power, but his cousin Max would not let him. Without waiting for Wilhelm to act, Max announced Wilhelm's abdication on November 9 and then resigned himself. Within hours, Philip Scheidermann, a socialist cabinet minister, publicly proclaimed Germany a republic. The next day, Wilhelm fled to neutral Netherlands. There he quietly lived out the last 23 years of his life. Ludendorff later said, "On November 9 Germany, lacking any firm hand, bereft of all will, robbed of her princes, collapsed like a house of cards."

While these changes were taking place, Prince Max's government was also negotiating a peace settlement with the Allies. On November 8, representatives of the German government met with General Foch and other Allied leaders to discuss Germany's surrender in the railroad carriage Foch used for his traveling headquarters. Over several days, they hammered out terms. The Germans were at a big disadvantage that made them want to come to an agreement quickly. Their army was not yet defeated but was steadily losing ground, and Germany itself was threatened with invasion. Germany was also threatened by the possibility of revolution that might become as radical as the Bolshevik Revolution in Russia. They had to act quickly.

Early in the morning of November 11, 1918, the German representatives signed an armistice agreement. Its terms called for cease-fire at 11:00 AM the same day—the 11th hour of the 11th day of the 11th month of the year. The news was joyously received in all the Allied nations and was greeted with quiet relief within Germany. Afterward, November 11, Armistice Day, was designated a national holiday in many Allied nations.

Public reactions to the armistice were joyous. Most servicemen eagerly planned what they would do when they got home. One American soldier, for example, said, "the first thing he was going to do was drink a gallon of milk. Another said he was going to eat ice cream until it came out of his ears." However, many servicemen found adjusting to sudden peace emotionally difficult. Malcolm Cowley, who

German prisoners captured by American troops in northern France in late September 1918.

Read a World War I-Era Adventure Novel

DURING THE EARLY 20th century there was no television, and both radio and movies were in their infancy. Consequently, books provided much of the entertainment children enjoyed. Especially popular were adventure stories with titles promising exciting thrills. World War I inspired

numerous adventure novels for young readers. Publishers issued such series as Air Service Boys, Army Boys, Boy Allies, and Navy Boys before the war was even over. Characters in already established series, such as Tom Swift, also went to war in new books. Most juvenile novels were aimed at boys, but girls were not entirely neglected. The Outdoor Girls helped in the war, too, and Nancy Drew's predecessor, Ruth Fielding, served as a wartime nurse in several novels.

Materials

✪ Computer connected to the Internet, or any electronic tablet device

✪ Pencil or pen

✪ Writing paper

Books published before 1923 have lost their copyright protection and are in the public domain. This means that electronic copies of many juvenile novels about the war can be easily obtained on the Internet for free. You can find downloadable text files of the books by searching individual

The 13 volumes of the Boy Allies series follow the exploits of two young Americans who fight with Allied army and naval units throughout the war. Written and published as the war progressed, each story is set amid real events and occasionally involves real people.

Collection of the author

titles or subjects such as "World War I juvenile novels." The best place to start, however, is Project Gutenberg's "World War I Bookshelf" at www .gutenberg.org/wiki/World_War_I_(Bookshelf). That page lists more than 30 juvenile titles, each of which you can download to read on a computer.

If you have an electronic device that enables you to read e-books, you can find dozens of juvenile novels at booksellers' websites either for free or for a modest charge. Before ordering a book for your tablet, make sure you have your parent's permission.

After you select and read a novel, draw on what you have learned about the war to answer questions such as these:

☆ Is the novel based on real events during the war?

☆ Does its action seem realistic? If not, why?

☆ Does it try to make war more glamorous and exciting than it really was?

☆ Is the book unfairly biased against the Central Powers? If so, in what ways?

☆ Does anything in the novel help you understand the war better?

had driven trucks and ambulances in France for the American Field Service, pointed out that many Allied airmen "had lived more intensely than they would ever live again and felt in a vague fashion that something in them had died on the eleventh of November, 1918. All the young men had been exposed to a variety of strong emotions. Their individualities had been affirmed, even in the anonymous disguise of a uniform." Cowley himself would go on to a long and distinguished career as a writer and literary critic.

Many sailors in the British and American navies were almost sorry that the war had ended. According to US secretary of the navy Josephus Daniels, "For a year, every officer and man in the Grand Fleet had been waiting and hoping for a chance to get at the Germans. And, at last, when that fleet surrendered, without striking a blow, their disappointment was too deep for words."

Meanwhile, the important thing was that combat was over. Fighting ended at the designated time, but the formal peace treaty would not come until several months later. Meanwhile, the Allies remained prepared for the possible resumption of fighting.

Americans celebrating news of the German surrender on New York City's Wall Street.

12

BEYOND THE ARMISTICE

T HE ARMISTICE STOPPED the killing in Europe and brought a sigh of relief to the whole world, but it did not formally end the war. Millions of armed troops remained deployed over the battlefields. They were ready to start fighting again if a formal peace agreement was not worked out. The armistice did, however, require Germany to undertake several drastic actions. All its troops in Belgium, Luxembourg, France, and Alsace-Lorraine had to return to Germany. The Germans immediately began withdrawing, leaving behind all their weapons, trucks, planes, and trains. Meanwhile, hundreds of thousands of Allied troops advanced into Germany to occupy the country and be ready if fighting resumed. They were the first armed Allied troops to enter Germany since the war had begun.

The armistice also required the German navy to surrender its ships to the Allies. Seventy-four vessels of the High Seas Fleet sailed to northern Scotland to be interned in the great bay of Scapa Flow, escorted by US and British warships. A British admiral afterward said, "It was a pitiful day to see those great ships coming in like sheep being herded by dogs to their fold, without an effort on anybody's part." Skeleton crews remained aboard the ships while peace negotiations began in France. In May 1919, it was announced that the peace settlement would reduce the German navy to a handful of ships and all other vessels would be permanently surrendered to the Allied nations. When Germany was given an ultimatum to sign the settlement or face a resumption of war, the German crews at Scapa Flow successfully scuttled all but 22 of their ships rather than surrender them. The gesture backfired on Germany, however. The peace settlement was modified to make Germany pay for the scuttled vessels with other ships.

The Paris Peace Conference

THE CONFERENCE convened in January 1919 to draw up formal peace settlement terms excluded Germany and its allies as well as Russia. Twenty-seven nations attended, but it was dominated by Britain, France, the United States, and Italy. The heads of government of

The Big Four Allied leaders at the Peace Conference in May 1919. Left to right: British prime minister David Lloyd George, Italian premier Vittorio Orlando, French premier Georges Clemenceau, and US president Woodrow Wilson.

those four nations attended in person and were popularly known as the Big Four.

Woodrow Wilson became the first US president to cross the Atlantic Ocean while in office when he sailed to France to attend the conference. He was received in Europe as a conquering hero. He was popular not only because he represented the nation that had made the difference in the war, but also because he championed the rights of all nations. In early 1918, he had publicly proclaimed a postwar settlement that would recognize 14 basic principles. His Fourteen Points stressed changes in international relations that would avoid the mistakes that had led to world war. His first point, for example, called for an end to secret diplomacy among nations and the principle that all international agreements should be undertaken in full public view. Wilson was less interested in punishing the losers in the war than he was in taking steps to ensure future peace.

Popular though Wilson was in Europe, his views were out of step with those of Britain, France, and Italy. Their leaders were less inclined to be conciliatory with the Central Powers. They wanted a settlement ensuring Germany would never start another war and making Germany pay dearly for the recent war. They were also concerned that some of Wilson's Fourteen Points would conflict with their own interests in foreign trade and overseas colonies.

The Treaty of Versailles

THE PARIS Peace Conference dragged on for six months as attendees debated and made compromises. Many of Wilson's Fourteen Points were incorporated in the final settlement, but he had to accept many compromises to get them in. His most important compromise was agreeing to harshly punitive terms for Germany.

The settlement was formally signed in the historic Palace of Versailles outside Paris on June 28, 1919—the fifth anniversary of Archduke Ferdinand's assassination. Facing the alternative of renewed war, Germany and its allies reluctantly signed the settlement.

The most important of the settlement's 440 separate articles were those pertaining to the dissolution of the Austro-Hungarian and Ottoman Empires and those punishing Germany. The punitive articles began with a clause in which Germany had to acknowledge full responsibility for the war. That, in turn, made it responsible for paying reparations for the Allied nations' losses. Germany also lost some of its own territory to its neighbors and was severely restricted in the size of its future military forces. The reparation bill imposed on Germany was equivalent to about $33 billion—an almost astronomical sum at that time. That requirement alone virtually ensured the failure of the peace settlement.

SUMMARY OF WILSON'S FOURTEEN POINTS

1. Reliance on open diplomacy rather than secret agreements
2. Freedom of the seas for all nations
3. Free trade for all nations
4. Greatest possible reduction of military forces and weapons in all nations
5. Fair readjustment of colonies
6. Allowing Russia to determine its own form of government
7. Respect for integrity of Belgium
8. Restoration of France's lost territory
9. Adjustment of Italy's borders based upon ethnicity
10. Fair development opportunities for Austria-Hungary
11. Independence for the Balkans' states
12. Self-determination for the peoples in the Ottoman Empire and free passage through Turkey's Dardanelles Strait
13. Polish independence
14. Formation of an international association of nations to guarantee the independence of all nations

The League of Nations and World War II

WILSON'S PROUDEST achievement at the conference was winning agreement to create the League of Nations. He was confident such an international body would prevent future wars. The league was formally created by the treaty and began meeting the following year in Geneva, Switzerland. Although the league was Wilson's brainchild, the United States never joined because the US Senate refused to ratify the treaty.

The league eventually failed because of its inability to prevent another world war. In 1946, after the second world war ended, it was replaced by the United Nations. The league's failure was almost guaranteed by the terms of the Treaty of Versailles. The harsh economic conditions imposed on Germany caused a negative backlash that made the treaty itself the object of German hostility. As early as 1922, Adolf Hitler gave a speech saying, "It cannot be that two million Germans should have fallen in vain.... No, we do not pardon, we demand—vengeance!" During the late 1920s, the Nationalist Socialist, or Nazi, Party, rose in Germany on the issue of the treaty. In 1933, Hitler, the leader of the party, became chancellor of Germany. Under his rule, Germany systematically undid all the restrictions the treaty had placed on it and went to start another world war.

The New Map of Europe

WELL BEFORE the armistice ended fighting on the western front in November 1918, the alliance of the Central Powers was falling apart. Bulgaria had joined the alliance in 1915 but had fared badly during the war. By mid-1918, the country was facing Allied occupation, nu-

Corporal Adolf Hitler (far left) with his army comrades during World War I. As a decorated veteran of World War I, Hitler felt a deep personal bitterness toward the Treaty of Versailles.

merous army desertions, a serious food crisis, and mass protests against the government. In late September, it signed its own armistice with the Allies and withdrew from the war. Its king abdicated in favor of his son shortly afterward.

German's primary ally, Austria-Hungary, made its peace with the Allies in late October. It then ordered its armies to retreat. That move began the breakup of the old empire. Hungary declared its independence from Austria on October 30. A few days later, Austria-Hungary no longer existed.

Poland, which had lost its independence during the late 18th century, began the war as a province of Russia. For that reason, many Polish army units fought for the Allies. However, during the war, Poland was occupied by both Germany and Austria-Hungary. Other Poles were forced to fight for the Central Powers. Some Polish units even fought against each other. As German and Austro-Hungarian control broke down, Poland declared itself an independent state in early October. Its borders later changed, but it has retained its independence into the 21st century.

An entirely new country that emerged from the war was the republic of Czechoslovakia. When it declared its independence in mid-October 1918, it combined Slavic Czech regions in Austria with Slavic Slovak regions in

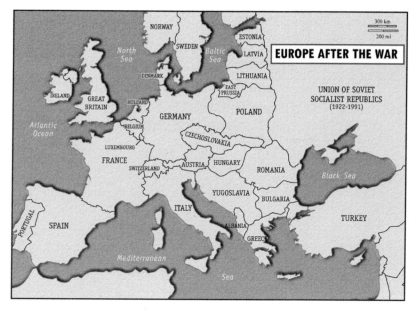

Hungary. The new country held together until 1993. That year it peacefully split into the Czech Republic and Slovakia.

Another new creation of the war was Yugoslavia in the Balkan region. Its emergence was slower than that of Czechoslovakia, but movements for its creation had a deeper history. The Serbs, Croats, and Slovenes declared their independence the moment they learned Austria-Hungary was out of the war.

Although a small area even by European standards, the Balkans had a complex mix of ethnic groups and an equally complex mix of political systems when World War I started. As chapter 1 explains, the war itself was triggered by the Serbian nationalist goal of joining Austria-Hungary's Balkan provinces to a greater Serbian Slavic state. The creation of Yugoslavia after the war was the realization of that goal. In late 1920, the independence of the Kingdom of Serbs, Croats, and Slovenes was formally recognized. In 1929, it changed its name to Yugoslavia, which means "southern Slavs." The new country held together for 70 years, but it was never a happy union because the region's long history of bitter ethnic rivalries was never resolved. After Yugoslavia's long-ruling dictator Josef Broz Tito died in 1980, old rivalries among Orthodox Christians, Roman Catholics, and Muslims started tearing the country apart. During the 1990s, these tensions developed into bloody civil wars that drew in American and western European military involvement. By the early 21st century, Yugoslavia had separated into its original parts: Serbia, Montenegro, Macedonia, Bosnia and Herzegovina, Slovenia, and Croatia. Had there been no World War I, those same countries might have come into existence with a great deal less bloodshed.

The Rise of the Soviet Union

THE COUNTRY most changed by the war was almost certainly Russia. Without the war, the old Russian imperial regime probably would not have lasted much longer. Impoverished and poorly governed, the Russian Empire was filled with peoples ready to revolt. The war may actually have helped keep the empire together a little longer than it otherwise might have lasted, as people pulled together against their common enemy. However, Russian involvement in the war was so poorly managed that conditions in the empire got even worse, and millions of people were killed. In the chaotic conditions surrounding Russia's military collapse, the most radical elements in the country took control and established a communist government that went on to build a new empire. After winning a civil war that may have killed even more people than World War I, Ilich Lenin's Bolshevik government created the Union of Soviet Socialist Republics in 1922.

The later history of that country is too complicated to explain here. Suffice it to say that the dictatorial government under Lenin's successor, Joseph Stalin, killed more people than did World War I, dominated eastern Europe after World War II, and entered into the Cold War rivalry with the United States that nearly led to the brink of yet another world war. However, despite the power that the Soviet Union eventually built up, it could not hold itself together any better than the old Russian Empire could. In 1991, the Soviet Union split into 15 independent republics. It is always dangerous

Visit a World War I Memorial

WORLD WAR I may have been honored by more memorials of various kinds than any other war. The war's huge toll in human lives and destruction made its survivors anxious to ensure the sacrifices of the war's victims were never forgotten. Europe has tens of thousands of World War I cemeteries, memorials, and museums. The American experience in the war was brief by comparison to what other nations had experienced. Its death toll was small by comparison, too. Nevertheless, many war memorials were built in the United States. Your challenge is to discover memorials located near your home and to visit at least one of them.

There is a good chance you may already be familiar with a nearby World War I memorial but are not aware of whom it honors. A number of famous football stadiums are examples. The University of California, University of Kansas, University of Nebraska, and University of Illinois all have "Memorial" stadiums named in honor of veterans and victims of the war. Los Angeles's famous Memorial Coliseum was also originally dedicated to World War I veterans. Memorial halls can be found in many cities and on many college campuses. Memorial parks, plazas, monuments, cemeteries, and even memorial schools can also be found.

Materials

- Computer with access to the Internet
- Public library

Locating memorials in your community may require imagination and legwork. If you have computer access to the Internet, try Google or Yahoo! searches such as these, substituting the name of a local town: "San Francisco"/"World War I" and "San Francisco"/"war memorial." Google searches of those exact terms will quickly lead to hits for San Francisco's War Memorial Opera House and several monuments to the war. If web searches fail to turn up anything nearby, visit the reference desk of your local public library and ask for help. Reference librarians can guide you to phone directories or other materials that should answer your questions.

After you locate a local memorial, pay it a visit. Examine it as closely as you can and look for features relating to the war, such as inscriptions and carved statues or reliefs. Talk about the site with your family and friends. Ask them if they know what it memorializes. Chances are they do not.

The closest thing to a national World War I memorial in the United States is the District of Columbia War Memorial. It stands on the edge of Washington, DC's National Mall, which has memorials to World War II, the Korean War, and the Vietnam War. Authorized by the US Congress in 1924, the DC Memorial was dedicated in 1931 to District of Columbia veterans of the Great War. Since 2008, there has been a movement to expand the memorial to honor all American veterans of the war.

Library of Congress LC-DIG-highsm-04253

to speculate about how history might have been different. Nevertheless, it is reasonable to say that without World War I, there may never have been a Soviet Union.

THE LAST LIVING VETERANS OF WORLD WAR I

As August 2014 marks the 100th anniversary of the outbreak of World War I, the only people still living who were directly touched by the war are centenarians who were too young during the war to remember it. In February 2012, the last known veteran of the war died in England. She was Florence Green, a nearly 111-year-old woman who had joined Britain's Royal Air Force in September 1918 at the age of 17. Over the two months remaining in the war, she worked as a waitress in an officers' mess hall at a base in England.

World War I's last known combatant, Claude Choules, died in Australia in May 2011 at the age of 110. At his death, he ranked as the both oldest man in Australia and the oldest man who had been born in Great Britain. When World War I began, he tried to join the British army as a bugler boy but was rejected because he was only 13 years old. In April 1915, when he was barely 14, he was accepted as a trainee in the Royal Navy. He finally saw active duty on a battleship in October 1917, when he was 16. He eventually spent 40 years in the navy. When he retired in 1956 at the age of 55, he could not have guessed that he still had half his life ahead of him.

The Mandate System

ONE OF the issues settled in the Paris Peace Conference was the fate of the former colonial territories of the German and Ottoman Empires. By the end of the war, all those territories had been occupied by Allied nations. These countries naturally wanted to add the territories to their own colonial empires, but doing so seemed to violate the principle of self-determination of peoples for which the war had been fought. A compromise was found. Instead of simply handing over the territories to their new occupiers, they were made "mandates" of the new League of Nations. In a sense, the league now owned the territories, and the countries to which they were mandated merely administered them as trustees.

Most of German East Africa was mandated to Great Britain, which renamed it Tanganyika. Two years after Tanganyika became independent in 1962, it merged with the island of Zanzibar to become Tanzania. The other parts of German East Africa, Ruanda-Urundi, later became independent as Rwanda and Burundi. Part of German Togoland was joined to Britain's Gold Coast colony. The rest was mandated to France as Togo. Part of German Kamerun was joined to British Nigeria. The rest was mandated to France as Cameroun. Most of the original colony was later reunited as the

independent republic of Cameroon. German Southwest Africa was mandated to the Union of South Africa. Germany's Pacific colonies were mandated to Japan, Australia, and New Zealand.

After the League of Nations dissolved, the United Nations assumed responsibility for overseeing the original mandate territories. Under its supervision, most of the former German colonies eventually gained independence. South Africa wanted to incorporate Southwest Africa into itself but was prevented by the United Nations. In 1990, Southwest Africa became independent as Namibia. After

World War II, the United States was awarded trusteeship over Germany's former Pacific island colonies that had earlier been given to Japan. Some of these islands, such as the Northern Marianas, are still under American administration.

The dissolution of the Ottoman Empire had similar consequences. Many Arabs had fought against the Turks in the hope of winning independence for their own people, but they were disappointed. Turkey's Middle Eastern territories were divided into mandates awarded to France and Britain. Under United Nations supervision, most of them did achieve

ABOVE: **American soldiers reunited with their wives meet their children born while they were in France.**

Keystone View Company

LEFT: **Happy American soldiers returning home from France. The suddenness with which the war ended found the United States unprepared to demobilize the millions of servicemen sent to Europe. Some men waited nearly 10 months to come home.**

National Archives and Records Administration

153

THE ONGOING "IRON HARVEST"

It has been estimated that during World War I an average of one ton of explosives fell on every square yard of ground along the trenches between Switzerland and the coast of Belgium. Although fighting ended in 1918, explosive weapons used there have never stopped killing. More than one-quarter of the artillery shells, bullets, grenades, and poison-gas canisters that fell sank into muddy and crumbling earth and disappeared from sight, waiting to explode later. Hundreds of people have been killed by them since 1918, and most of those munitions are still dangerous.

Every year, farmers plow up hundreds of tons of unexploded munitions while planting and harvesting crops. Their annual "iron harvests" have become so routine that the farmers simply leave explosives they find next to their fields for special government agencies to collect and dispose of.

All rusting and disintegrating munitions are dangerous, but canisters containing poisonous gases are especially dangerous because they can remain toxic long after explosives have lost their effectiveness. As recently as 2001, two entire French towns were evacuated when World War I mustard gas collected for disposal started to leak.

independence after World War II. Palestine's status was complicated by the presence of a large number of Jewish residents who proclaimed the state of Israel there in 1948.

The Cost of the War

EXAMINING WHAT the war cost in human lives will help put other subjects in perspective. Estimates of the war's death toll cannot be exact. Not all the countries kept accurate records. Moreover, it is not always clear whether many deaths were caused by the war or something else. At least five million Allied military personnel died from battlefield wounds or other causes. The Central Powers lost about four million military personnel, about half of whom were Germans. Among the Allies, France and Russia suffered the most deaths.

Figures for civilian deaths are even less precise. Direct military action killed just under one million civilians in all countries. The numbers of civilians killed by starvation, accidents, and diseases spread by the war were much higher. The Allied nations lost nearly three million civilians to such causes. The Central Powers may have lost more than four million civilians, mostly in the Ottoman Empire.

Overall, at least 16 million human beings died because of the war. Countless others endured serious wounds, injuries, illnesses, and other afflictions from the war. Many lost their homes, farms, businesses, and livelihoods. By any measure, the war caused more human suffering than any war up to its time.

Early postcard view of northern France's Neuville-St Vaast German war cemetery, which now contains the graves of more than 44,000 German soldiers killed on the western front. There are nearly 1,000 World War I cemeteries in France alone.

Design a Commemorative Postage Stamp

NATIONS FREQUENTLY REMEMBER important events and people in their history by issuing commemorative postage stamps in their honor. The centennial anniversary of World War I is certain to inspire many nations to issue commemoratives from 2014 to 2018. Collecting those stamps would be both fun and educational. For now, however, you can design a World War I commemorative stamp yourself.

Materials

- ✪ Computer with Internet access (optional)
- ✪ Art paper
- ✪ Pencil
- ✪ Drawing and painting tools of your choice

US commemorative stamp issued in 1985.

Collection of the author

If you are not already familiar with commemorative stamps, you can easily study examples on the Internet. Using a computer web browser, search "commemorative stamps" and then click on "Images" to bring up the illustrations on the screen. Notice the standard elements in each commemorative stamp:

- ☆ country name
- ☆ price of stamp
- ☆ subject commemorated
- ☆ illustration

Many commemoratives also have the date of the event being observed. For example, the 1964 French stamp illustrated in chapter 2 of this book commemorates the 50th anniversary of the Allied victory in the First Battle of the Marne in 1914. The stamp is illustrated with pictures of the famous taxi cabs used to transport troops to the front during that battle.

Give some thought to the subject you would like to see commemorated on a stamp. It could be an event, such as the Battle of Jutland or the sinking of the *Lusitania*; a person, such as Alvin York, Edith Cavell, or Germany's Red Baron; or a more general subject, such as the victims of the war, messenger dogs, or the naval convoy system. Many of these subjects are likely to be depicted in real centennial stamps. Try to think of a subject that deserves being on a stamp but probably will not be, such as the horses that died in the war. After you select your subject and decide what country's stamp it will go on, sketch out some rough designs in pencil. When you find one you like, use your favorite drawing instruments to complete the design.

RESOURCES

Key Personalities of World War I

Albert I (1875–1934) King of Belgium who is considered one of the Allied Powers' heroes of the war for his resistance to Germany's 1914 invasion and for commanding the Allied reconquest of Belgium's coast in 1918.

Edmund Allenby (1861–1936) British general who commanded Allied forces in the Middle East from 1917 to 1919; later British high commissioner in Egypt (1919–1935).

Edith Cavell (1865–1915) British nurse working in Belgium who was executed by Germany for helping Allied prisoners to escape.

Winston S. Churchill (1874–1965) British politician who as first lord of the Admiralty in 1915 championed the ultimately disastrous Gallipoli campaign. He was minister of munitions in 1917 and secretary for war from 1919 to 1921. Best known as prime minister through World War II.

Georges Clemenceau (1841–1929) French prime minister in 1906–1909 and 1917–1920; presided over the postwar peace conference and pushed for harsh terms for Germany.

Franz Ferdinand (1863–1914) Austrian archduke and heir to the Austrian throne whose assassination triggered the war.

Ferdinand Foch (1851–1929) French army general who held several command positions through the war until April 1918, when he was appointed commander in chief of all Allied forces.

George V (1865–1936) King of Great Britain throughout the war.

Douglas Haig (1861–1928) Chief British army commander who succeeded General French in western Europe in 1915–1917.

Paul Ludwig Hans von Hindenburg (1847–1934) Supreme commander of the German army through most of the war. After the war served as president from 1925 to 1934.

John Rushworth Jellicoe (1859–1935) British admiral who commanded the Great Fleet in 1914–1916, served as First Sea Lord in 1916–1917, and was made admiral of the fleet in 1919.

Joseph Joffre (1852–1931) French general who as the first supreme French commander in 1915–1916 pushed for strong and often costly offensives.

Franz Joseph (1830–1916) Last ruler of the Austria-Hungary Empire.

Horatio Herbert Kitchener (1850–1916) Britain's most distinguished army commander before the war, served as secretary of state for war in 1914–1916. His image was used extensively in military recruitment posters.

Thomas Edward Lawrence (1888–1935) British scholar of the Middle East and army officer who helped organize and direct the Arab revolt against Turkish rule in 1916–1918.

Vladimir Ilyich Lenin (1870–1925) Russian revolutionary leader who as head of the Bolsheviks took Russia out of the war in late 1917 and led the creation of the Union of Soviet Socialist Republics.

Paul Emil von Lettow-Vorbeck (1870–1964) Commander of German forces in German East Africa (now mainland Tanzania), where he directed guerrilla operations that tied up Allied forces until after the 1918 armistice.

David Lloyd George (1863–1945) British politician who held several ministerial posts during the war until 1916, when he became prime minister, a position he held until 1922.

Erich von Ludendorff (1865–1937) German general who served as Hindenburg's chief of staff through most of the war and played a leading role in planning German offensives.

Helmuth Johannes Ludwig von Moltke (1848–1916) German general who modified the Schlieffen Plan in the first great offensive of the war and was removed from command when it failed.

Nicholas II (1869–1918) Last Russian tsar (emperor), whose assumption of command of military forces in mid-1915 proved disastrous. Forced to abdicate by the Russian Revolution in 1917 and killed, with his entire family, the following year.

Vittorio Emanuele Orlando (1860–1952) Italian politician who became prime minister in late 1917 and represented Italy in the postwar peace conference.

Wilfred Owen (1893–1918) British poet and soldier who was killed in action exactly one week before the armistice.

John Joseph Pershing (1860–1948) General who commanded the American Expeditionary Force, which he steadfastly insisted on preserving as an autonomous component among the Allied armies. After the war, he became US chief of staff.

Henri-Philippe Pétain (1856–1951) French general credited with saving Verdun from a German offensive in 1916 who was French commander in chief by early 1918. His reputation as a war hero was ruined in World War II, when he collaborated with the German occupation of France.

Gavrilo Princip (1894–1918) Bosnian Serb who, acting as an agent of a radical Serbian nationalist organization, assassinated Austrian archduke Franz Ferdinand on June 28, 1914. He died from tuberculosis in prison.

Manfred Richthofen (1892–1918) Ace German pilot credited with shooting down 80 enemy planes, the most of all pilots during the war. Nicknamed the Red Baron because of the red triplane he frequently flew.

Edward Rickenbacker (1890–1973) Top American ace aviator during the war.

Jan Christian Smuts (1870–1950) South African military and political leader who had fought against Britain during the South African War (1899–1902) but supported Britain in both world wars. In 1914–1915, he led a column against German positions in Southwest Africa. In 1916–1917, he commanded British operations against Lettow-Vorbeck in German East Africa. He later became prime minister of the Union of South Africa.

Maximilian von Spee (1861–1914) German naval officer who commanded a squadron that raided Allied shipping in the South Atlantic and Pacific Oceans in 1914 until defeated and killed by a British squadron at the Falkland Islands.

Alfred von Tirpitz (1849–1930) German admiral credited with building his country's modern navy before the war. Believing the surface fleet was unready when the war began, he advocated unrestricted submarine warfare and resigned in early 1916 when his ideas were ignored.

Wilhelm (William) II (1859–1941) Hereditary king of Prussia and emperor of Germany. Despite being related to the royal families of Britain and Russia, he was a fervent advocate of war. He generally allowed his generals to direct military operations but was responsible for keeping his navy's High Seas Fleet in port. After abdicating two days before the Armistice, he retired to the Netherlands.

Woodrow Wilson (1856–1924) President of the United States, 1913–1921. Although Wilson was a leading advocate of keeping America out of the war during his first term, he led the country to war early in his second term. After the war, he played a major role in the postwar peace conference and led the movement to create the League of Nations.

Alvin York (1887–1964) American war hero who single-handedly killed about 20 Germans and took 132 prisoners.

Ferdinand von Zeppelin (1838–1917) German inventor who developed the rigid airships named after him.

Websites for Further Exploration

Project Gutenberg: World War I Bookshelf
www.gutenberg.org/wiki/World_War_I_ (Bookshelf)
Project Gutenberg offers free downloads of electronic texts of public domain books. This page lists hundreds of books about the war that can be accessed in minutes. Arranged under broad headings, the titles include many juvenile novels.

Library of Congress Prints & Photographs Online Catalog
www.loc.gov/pictures
This federal government agency makes available to the public thousands of free digital files of out-of-copyright photos from the war. Finding specific pictures requires using a variety of search terms, such as "World War I," "First World War," "Great War," and names of specific people and battles. Searching for "World War I posters" will yield a particularly rich trove of full-color images.

The Great War, 1914–1918
www.nationalarchives.gov.uk/education/greatwar
British national archives site about the war with questions and answers designed for classroom use. Includes a teacher's guide.

Documents of World War I
www.mtholyoke.edu/acad/intrel/ww1.htm
This Mt. Holyoke College web page has links to hundreds of important contemporary documents, plus links to other useful World War I websites.

The World War I Document Archive

wwi.lib.byu.edu

Maintained by the Brigham Young University Library, this site has links to thousands of wartime documents and images arranged under headings such as "Diaries, Memorials, Personal Reminiscences," "Books, Special Topics and Commentaries," and "Documents by Year."

BBC News: The Great War, Eighty Years On

news.bbc.co.uk/2/hi/special_report/1998/10/98/world_war_i/197437.stm

This British site has links to many contemporary documents, including letters written by soldiers. Of special interest are its recordings of old radio interviews with participants in the war. Additional material can be found on the BBC's History pages at www.bbc.co.uk/history/worldwars/wwone.

World War I: Trenches on the Web—An Internet History of the Great War

www.worldwar1.com

This site caters to people interested in paid tours of wartime sites, but it also has several search engines that lead to substantial historical information.

Lost Poets of the Great War

www.english.emory.edu/LostPoets/index.html

This Emory University website has a narrow focus and includes profiles of John McCrae, Wilfred Owen, Isaac Rosenberg, Alan Seeger, and Edward Thomas.

War Times Journal: Great War Series

www.wtj.com/wars/greatwar

This site offers information on war games related to historical events but also has links to many useful documents, texts of complete books, and articles about World War I.

firstworldwar.com: A Multimedia History of World War One

www.firstworldwar.com

Another site with links to many useful documents and articles. Of greatest interest, however, are the site's numerous links to pictures, maps, films, and information about specific battlefields, cemeteries, museums, and memorials.

History: World War I

www.history.com/topics/world-war-i

These History channel pages contain a variety of multimedia features, including film clips, photo galleries, and recordings of contemporary speeches.

Spartacus Education: The First World War

www.spartacus.schoolnet.co.uk/FWW.htm

Free British online encyclopedia with a wealth of well-organized links to many hundreds of articles on specific subjects, both narrow and broad. The page on trench warfare alone has links to 70 illustrated articles on specialized topics.

British Pathé: Selected Footage of World War I

www.britishpathe.com/workspaces/rgallagher/Selected-footage-of-World-War-I

Selection of fascinating film clips shot during the war, including vivid footage of German troops going "over the top" from their trench position while being shelled.

The Great War and the Shaping of the 20th Century

www.pbs.org/greatwar

PBS website with multimedia material connected with public television's documentary series of the same title.

Notable Feature Films About World War I

SOME OF the best films about World War I were made during the silent-film era. Although they may seem old-fashioned to modern audiences, those early films are well worth watching. Because movies about heroic pilots fighting in the sky are visually more exciting than movies about soldiers in trenches, a large number of World War I films are about the aerial war. Keep in mind, therefore, that many aspects of World War I have not been adequately depicted in films.

The African Queen (1951) PG Adaptation of C. S. Forester's novel about a missionary woman and an Englishman who sail a boat called the *African Queen* down a river in the hope of sinking a German steamer patrolling a great central African lake. The story and geography are imaginary, but the film nevertheless shows what German East Africa was like during the war.

All Quiet on the Western Front (1930) Unrated First and best of several adaptations of German author Erich Marie Remarque's classic novel about German boys persuaded by their patriotic schoolmaster to enlist in the army, only to encounter misery and despair. This is one of the greatest of all antiwar films.

The Big Parade (1925) Unrated One of the most successful silent films of its time, this movie is about a rich young American man who joins the army and is transformed by what he experiences while fighting in France. Offers a grim view of trench warfare.

The Blue Max (1966) Unrated British film about a German soldier (George Peppard) who transfers to the air service and becomes obsessed with earning the "Blue Max" medal given to ace pilots. This is not a terribly realistic treatment of the war, but it offers exciting air combat scenes.

Darling Lili (1970) G An American musical in which a British singer (Julie Andrews) works as a spy for Germany until she falls in love with an American pilot (Rock Hudson). It is another not very realistic film about the war but does include exciting scenes of aerial combat.

The Dawn Patrol (1938) Unrated Realistic American film about British Royal Flying Corps pilots struggling to keep up with an elite enemy squadron at a moment when the Germans held air superiority. This is a remake of a 1930 film with the same title.

Doughboys (1930) Unrated Amusing early sound film in which the great silent film comedian Buster Keaton plays a rich loafer who accidentally enlists in the US Army and ends up fighting in the trenches.

The Eagle and the Hawk (1933) Unrated Dramatic film about Britain's Royal Flying Corps, in which Frederic March and Cary Grant play pilots struggling to deal with the grim realities of the war. One of the screenwriters was the American RFC pilot Bogart Rogers.

A Farewell to Arms (1957) Unrated Adapted from Ernest Hemingway's 1929 novel based on his own experiences as a volunteer ambulance driver in Italy, this film revolves around a fictional American ambulance driver (Rock Hudson) who falls in love with a nurse (Jennifer Jones) and offers a glimpse of the Italian theater of the war.

Flyboys (2006) PG-13 Loosely based on the experiences of real American pilots, this film starring James Franco is about 38 young Americans who volunteer to fly in France's Lafayette Escadrille before the United States officially entered the war.

Gallipoli (1981) PG This Australian film starring Mel Gibson is about young Australian men sent to Turkey to fight in the Allies' disastrous Gallipoli campaign.

Grand Illusion (*La Grande Illusion*, 1937) Unrated Considered one of the greatest films ever made, this French production is about French prisoners of war trying to escape from their German captors. It contains no scenes of actual warfare but deals with larger questions about the morality of war.

Hell's Angels (1930) Unrated The first great action film of the sound era, this American film about British pilots is filled with spectacular aerial combat scenes.

Joyeux Noel (2005) Unrated French film about the unofficial truce that ordinary British, French, and German troops called on Christmas day in 1914.

King of Hearts (1966) Unrated This gentle film is about a British soldier sent to a French town to deactivate a bomb the Germans are believed to have planted. The only people he finds there are inmates of an insane asylum who seem to be more sane than the soldiers fighting the war.

Lawrence of Arabia (1962) PG This is a spectacular epic production about the role of T. E. Lawrence (played by Peter O'Toole) in the Arab revolt against Turkish rule in Mesopotamia. It is easily the best film about the desert war.

The Lighthorsemen (1987) PG Another film about the desert war in Mesopotamia, this Australian production is about a real incident in the war when Australian light cavalrymen captured a strongly defended Turkish position.

The Lost Battalion (2001) Unrated Made-for-television film about the American battalion that was cut off from other Allied units and surrounded by Germans during the Battle of the Argonne in 1918.

Oh! What a Lovely War (1969) G Adapted from a stage play, this British musical covers the entire history of the war, taking every opportunity to call attention to its most foolish aspects—including the reasons the war started.

The Red Baron (2008) PG-13 Made in the English language, this German film about Baron von Richthofen is heavily fictionalized and depicts Richthofen as more peace-loving than he was known to have been. Nevertheless, it uses computer-generated imagery (CGI) to create very exciting aerial combat scenes.

The Road to Glory (1936) Unrated American film about a French regiment fighting on the western front in 1916. Provides a good depiction of conditions in the trenches.

Sergeant York (1941) Unrated This is a highly fictionalized account of the American war hero Alvin York's life, but it contains a reasonably accurate depiction of his exploits during the war. Gary Cooper won an Oscar for his portrayal of York.

Shoulder Arms (1918) Unrated One of Charlie Chaplin's most popular short films, this silent movie provides a very funny look at a soldier's life in the trenches.

War Horse (2011) PG-13 Adapted from a children's novel by British writer Michael Morpurgo, this film follows the horrible experiences of a thoroughbred horse that goes through many owners after being taken to France by a British cavalry officer. Meanwhile, the horse's original owner joins the British army in the hope of being reunited with his horse.

What Price Glory? (1952) Unrated This not terribly funny comedy with James Cagney is about US Marines. It is worth watching because it is set in the period when the first American troops sent overseas were training in France before entering combat.

Wings (1927) PG-13 This film about two American fighter pilots in the war was the first movie to win a best picture Oscar (in 1929). The film was made by a team of veteran World War I pilots and used real airplanes for its outstanding aerial combat scenes.

NOTES

Chapter 1: The Road to War

"The effect of the war upon the United States" www.firstworldwar.com

Chapter 2: Stalemate on the Western Front

"Patriotism is not enough" Mitchell, *Monstrous Regiment*, 375
"Every effort must be made" Willmott, *World War I*, 39
"Dulce et Decorum Est" Ward, *World War One British Poets*, 21
"It was absolutely astounding" Ellis, *Eye-Deep in Hell*, 172
"People out here seem to think" Willmott, *World War I*, 99

Chapter 3: Trench Warfare

"No one who was not there" Ellis, *Eye-Deep in Hell*, 51
"That waiting around before you go" Rendinell, *One Man's War*, 147
"the immense amount of decay" Allen, *Toward the Flame*, 112
"A diabolical uproar surrounds us" Ellis, *Eye-Deep in Hell*, 63
"the whole world was coming to an end" Hallas, *Doughboy War*, 174
"Though food was abundant" Ranlett, *Let's Go*, 102
"At night, the boys would take off" Duane, *Dear Old "K,"* 23–24
"didn't have ventilating systems" Hallas, *Doughboy War*, 63
"there are thousands of 'em " Van Emden, *Tommy's Ark*, 166

"I was walking down the trench" Wise, *A Marine Tells It to You*, 183–184
"Flies—millions and millions of them" *120th Field Artillery Diary*, 224

Chapter 4: Other Fronts

"sick man of Europe" Haythornthwaite, *World War One Source Book*, 299
"lion-hearted courage" Hough, *The Great War at Sea*, 167

Chapter 5: The Weapons of War

"barbed wire . . . is a dreadful handicap" Jacks, *Service Record*, 112–113
"One never saw soldiers with beards" Clarke, *Over There*, 67–68
"We were told of the value of horses" De la Mater, *The Story of Battery B*, 29
"gas mask pains and miseries begin" *120th Field Artillery Diary*, 222
"We were all absolutely flabbergasted" Willmott, *World War I*, 167

Chapter 6: The War at Sea

"quite homeless" Hough, *The Great War at Sea*, 96
"Our one desire" Hough, *The Great War at Sea*, 290
"I give your Majesty my word" Meyer, *A World Undone*, 482

Chapter 7: The War in the Air

"attracted the adventurous" Lewis, *Sagittarius Rising*, 137

"I'd rather die as an aviator" Longstreet, *The Canvas Falcons*, 234

"Ah, so what" Longstreet, *The Canvas Falcons*, 44–45

"when a number of machines" Lewis, *Sagittarius Rising*, 169

"London, the heart" Longstreet, *The Canvas Falcons*, 124

Chapter 8: Animals Go to War

"Well, sir, how would you feel" Van Emden, *Tommy's Ark*, 244

"one of the beastliest things" Van Emden, *Tommy's Ark*, 180

"Do you remember me telling you" Van Emden, *Tommy's Ark*, 102–103

"If anything speaks of home" Van Emden, *Tommy's Ark*, 154

"they do not know where they are" Howe, *Memoirs of the Harvard Dead*, 4:426

"One amusing feature" Van Emden, *Tommy's Ark*, 83

Chapter 9: Enter the United States

"Thank goodness I've seen a bit" Farwell, *Over There*, 262–263

"He kept us out of war" Venzon, *United States in the First World War*, 796

"Stand firm in armed neutrality" Carlisle, *World War I*, 212

"visions of being rushed" Thomas, *Woodfill of the Regulars*, 291

"Over There" sheet music (New York: Leo. Feist, 1917)

"triumphal procession" Hallas, *Doughboy War*, 31–32

"Frenchman raised his cap and waved" DuPuy, *Machine Gunner's Notes*, 50

"that it would be nice to capture" Hoffman, *I Remember the Last War*, 105

Chapter 10: The Home Fronts

"the best pleasures of life" Ellis, *Eye-Deep in Hell*, 158

Chapter 11: Ending the Fighting

"Do not trust the promises" Willmott, *World War I*, 207

"After the censor had finished" Wilson & Tooze, *With the 364th Infantry*, 33

"Tables in the kitchen" Macdonald, *To the Last Man*, 143

"a gang of the toughest" Hallas, *Doughboy War*, 20

"On November 9 Germany" Willmott, *World War I*, 286

"the first thing he was going to do" Hallas, *Doughboy War*, 322

"had lived more intensely" Longstreet, *The Canvas Falcons*, 355

"For a year, every officer and man" Farwell, *Over There*, 263

Chapter 12: Beyond the Armistice

"It was a pitiful day" Farwell, *Over There*, 263

"It cannot be that" Keegan, *The First World War*, 3

GLOSSARY

ALL TERMS are defined as they were used during World War I, except as otherwise explained.

abdication Renouncing one's position of power.

ace Fighter pilot who downs a certain number of enemy planes.

airship Any lighter-than-air craft that can be powered and steered. See also *observation balloons*.

Allied Powers (Allies) Nations fighting against the Central Powers that initially included Great Britain, France, Belgium, Russia, Italy, and Japan. The United States later became an "associated" member, and Russia dropped out.

American Expeditionary Force (AEF) US Army and Marine troops who served in France.

armistice Truce to end hostilities, with a formal peace treaty to come later.

Armistice Day US holiday commemorating the end of fighting on November 11, 1918; renamed Veterans Day in 1947 to commemorate veterans of all wars.

artillery Guns too large to be carried by individual soldiers, including howitzers, mortars, and cannons, that could be mounted either in fixed positions or on moving carriages or ships.

Austria-Hungary Old empire encompassing what are now Austria, Hungary, and several neighboring territories until it was dissolved by World War I.

Balkans Peninsula separating the Adriatic and Black Seas. The region now encompasses all or most of Albania, Bosnia and Herzegovina, Bulgaria, Croatia, Greece, Kosovo, Macedonia, Montenegro, and Serbia; and parts of Italy, Romania, Slovenia, and Turkey.

barrage Heavy concentration of artillery fire against one area.

battle cruiser Large warship more lightly armed and armored but faster than a battleship.

battleship Largest and most heavily armed and armored class of warship.

bayonet Blade attached to the end of a rifle barrel for use in hand-to-hand fighting.

Big Four French prime minister Georges Clemenceau, British prime minister David Lloyd George, Italian prime minster Vittorio Emanuele Orlando, and US president Woodrow Wilson, who together dominated the 1919 postwar peace conference.

biplane Airplane with two sets of wings, one above the other.

blockade, naval Used of warships to prevent vessels from entering or leaving enemy ports.

Bolshevik Member of the most extreme faction of Russian communists who seized power in November 1917.

British Expeditionary Force (BEF) First British army troops sent to France in 1914.

camouflage Disguising of vehicles, planes, ships, or troops to make them more difficult for enemies to see.

casualties Military personnel unable to serve because of death, wounds, sickness, capture, or becoming missing in action. Battle "losses" are usually measured in "casualties," not deaths.

cavalry Troops trained to do most of their marching and fighting mounted on animals, usually horses.

Central Powers Taking their name from their position between France and Russia, the countries opposing the Allied Powers: Germany, Austria-Hungary, Turkey, and Bulgaria. See also *Triple Alliance*.

chemical warfare Use of toxic liquids, gases, and solids as weapons.

combatant nation Country directly involved in fighting.

conscientious objector Person refusing induction into military service because of personal, religious, or moral objections to violence.

convoy system Clustering of merchant ships to sail under naval escort to reduce danger of enemy—especially submarine—attack.

demobilization Postwar process of releasing personnel from military service. See also *mobilization*.

destroyer Small and fast warship that was a primary weapon against submarines.

dirigible Rigidly framed airship that could be steered, such as a zeppelin.

division Army unit containing about 10,000 troops in European forces and about 20,000 troops in the US Army.

dogfight Aerial combat among two or more aircraft.

doughboy Friendly nickname for US infantrymen in Europe.

dreadnought Class of large, fast battleships armed only with large guns.

eastern front War zone between Russia in the east and Germany and Austria-Hungary in the west.

empire Geographically large political unit encompassing diverse peoples or territories under a single sovereign ruler, usually known as an emperor.

flank Right or left side of a military formation that was often the focus of enemy attack.

Fourteen Points Terms outlined by President Wilson in early 1918 for a settlement of the war (see sidebar on page 147).

gas mask Portable device designed to protect its wearer from inhaling toxic gases.

High Seas Fleet Core of the Germany navy that at its peak comprised 27 modern battleships and battle cruisers and many smaller vessels.

home front Broad term for civilian populations in areas that may be far from armed conflict.

howitzer artillery weapon designed to fire shells short distances in a high trajectory.

Hun Uncomplimentary Allied nickname for a German; recalls the allegedly barbaric Huns of the early Middle Ages who helped destroy the Roman Empire.

infantry Soldiers who march and fight on their feet, in contrast to cavalry soldiers.

kaiser Title of German emperors derived from the Roman word *caesar* used for emperors. See also *tsar*.

League of Nations International organization created after the war with the goal of resolving conflicts before they could escalate into wars.

machine gun Heavy but nonetheless portable firearm capable of continuous and rapid fire from mounts on ground, moving vehicles, airplanes, and vessels.

mine Explosive weapon designed to detonate when touched by objects moving over it. Land mines are planted under the surface of the ground; marine mines are anchored to float just under the surface of the water.

mining Driving of tunnels for the purpose of placing explosives below enemy trenches.

mobilization Preparation of a national military force for war. See also *demobilization*.

morale Confidence and positive emotional condition of a person or group, such as a military unit.

mortar Small artillery gun that fired shells at even higher trajectories than howitzers to drop into very close enemy positions, such as trenches.

mustard gas Toxic mist that caused blindness, skin blistering, and often fatal poisoning.

neutral nation Independent country not formally allied with either side during the war.

no-man's-land Centuries-old term popularized during World War I to describe the dangerous, often battered, and usually narrow ground separating enemy trenches.

observation balloon Gas-filled balloon used to raise reconnaissance observers high above the ground or sea while tethered to the ground or a ship.

offensive Organized and typically large-scale attack on an enemy position.

Ottoman Empire Turkish-ruled empire dating back to the early 14th century that controlled parts of the Balkan Peninsula and much of the Middle East at the start of the war.

pandemic Health epidemic of global proportions.

propaganda Information—which may be true or false—distributed to increase support for one side in a conflict while discrediting the opposing side.

rationing Government-managed allocation of limited resources, such as food items, fuels, and materials for clothing.

reconnaissance Search for information about enemy positions on either land or sea through direct observation.

reparations, war Postwar payments made by the losers to the winners to compensate for wartime damages.

reserves Troops held back from battle until needed.

Royal Navy Formal name of Great Britain's naval arm.

Schlieffen Plan Large-scale German war plan developed before 1905 by General Count Alfred von Schlieffen (1833–1913). It called for a speedy conquest of France by going through Belgium, followed by rapid movement by train of troops to take on Russia in the east.

Serbians (Serbs) Southern Slavs living throughout the Balkans, with their heaviest concentrations in Serbia and Bosnia Herzegovina.

shell (1) Projectile fired by a cannon or other artillery weapon containing an explosive charge designed to burst on hitting its target. (2) Bullet fired by a rifle or other small firearm.

Slavs Eastern European peoples who speak closely related Slavic languages and share other cultural traits. They include Russians, Bulgarians, Croatians, Czechs, Poles, Serbs (Serbians), Slovaks, Slovenes, and Ukrainians.

strategy The broadest plans and aims behind decisions of military leaders, in contrast to tactics.

tactics Manner in which military forces are used in individual combat situations, in contrast to broader decisions involved in strategy.

tank Armored combat vehicle propelled by caterpillar tracks instead of wheels.

torpedo Self-propelled underwater projectile designed to explode on contact with an enemy vessel.

trench foot Serious foot ailment, similar in its effects to frostbite, afflicting trench soldiers standing too long in cold water.

trench warfare Broad term for the essentially static situation that developed on the western front and in some other sectors of the war in which most of the fighting was done by combat units confined to underground trenches.

Triple Alliance Late-19th-century military alliance among Germany, Austria-Hungary, and Italy. Germany and Austria-Hungary continued the alliance to form the Central Powers during the war, but Italy renounced it and later joined the Allied Powers.

Triple Entente Military alliance among France, Great Britain, and Russia formed in 1904 to counter the Triple Alliance.

tsar (czar) Title of Russian emperors, which like the German kaiser, derived from the Roman word *caesar*.

U-boat German term for a submarine from German *Unterseeboot* for "undersea boat."

Versailles, Treaty of Peace treaty formally ending World War I that was first signed on June 28, 1919. The United States never signed the treaty and made its own peace agreement with Germany in 1921.

war of attrition Wartime situation in which enemies are unable to defeat each other outright and instead wear each other down until one side either collapses or gives up in exhaustion.

western front Combat zone mainly in northern France and Belgium in which most of the land fighting between Germany and France and Great Britain was concentrated throughout the war.

zeppelin German name for dirigibles that were originally built by Count Ferdinand von Zeppelin.

BIBLIOGRAPHY

☆ Denotes titles most suitable for young readers.

☆ Adams, Simon. *Eyewitness World War I*. New York: DK Publishing, 2007.

Albrecht-Carrié, René. *The Meaning of the First World War*. Englewood Cliffs, NJ: Prentice-Hall, 1965.

Allen, Hervey. *Toward the Flame: A Memoir of World War I*. New York: Farrar & Rinhart, 1926.

☆ Atwood, Kathryn. *Women Heroes of World War I*. Chicago: Chicago Review Press, 2014.

Axelrod, Alan. *The Complete Idiot's Guide to World War I*. New York: Alpha Books, 2000.

Barbeau, Arthur E., and Florette Henri. *The Unknown Soldiers: African-American Troops in World War I*. New York: Da Capo, 1996.

Brown, Malcolm. *The Imperial War Museum Book of the First World War: A Great Conflict Recalled in Previously Unpublished Letters, Diaries, Documents, and Memoirs*. Norman: University of Oklahoma Press, 1993.

Burg, David F., and L. Edward Purcell. *Almanac of World War I*. Lexington: University of Kentucky Press, 1998.

Carlisle, Rodney P. *World War I* (Eyewitness History series). New York: Facts On File, 2006.

Clarke, William F. *Over There with O'Ryan's Roughnecks: Reminiscences of a Private. . .* Seattle: Superior, 1968.

Corrigan, Gordon. *Mud, Blood, and Poppycock: Britain and the First World War*. London: Cassell, 2004.

Cross, Wilbur. *Zeppelins of World War I*. New York: Barnes & Noble, 1991.

De la Mater, Roswell. *The Story of Battery B, 306th F.A.* New York: Premier, 1919.

☆ Deary, Terry, and Martin Brown. *The Frightful First World War and the Woeful Second World War: Two Horrible Books in One*. London: Scholastic Books, 2000.

Duane, James T. *Dear Old "K."* Boston: author, 1922.

DuPuy, Charles M. *A Machine Gunner's Notes: France 1918*. Pittsburgh, PA: Reed & Witting, 1920.

Ellis, John. *Eye-Deep in Hell: Trench Warfare in World War I*. New York: Pantheon Books, 1976.

✩ Farmer, Gene, and Editors of *Life*, eds. *The First World War*. New York: Time, Inc., 1965.

Farwell, Byron. *The Great War in Africa, 1914–1918*. New York: Norton, 1986.

Farwell, Bryon. *Over There: The United States in the Great War*. New York: Norton, 1999.

✩ Forty, Simon, ed. *World War I: A Visual Encyclopedia*. London: PRC, 2002.

Fussell, Paul. *The Great War and Modern Memory*. New York: Oxford University Press, 1977.

Gilbert, Martin. *Atlas of World War I*. 2d ed. New York: Oxford University Press, 1994.

✩ Goldstein, Donald M., and Harry J. Maihafer. *America in World War I: The Story and Photographs*. Washington, DC: Potomac Books, 2004.

✩ Gosling, Lucinda. *Brushes & Bayonets: Cartoons, Sketches, and Paintings of World War I*. London: Osprey, 2008.

✩ Granfield, Linda. *Where Poppies Grow: A World War I Companion*. Brighton, MA: Fitzhenry & Whiteside, 2001.

Greenwald, Maurine Weiner. *Women, War, and Work: The Impact of World War I on Women Workers in the United States*. Ithaca, NY: Cornell University Press, 1990.

✩ Hallas, James H., ed. *Doughboy War: The American Expeditionary Force in World War I*. Mechanicsburg, PA: Stackpole Books, 2009.

Haythornwaite, Philip J. *The World War One Source Book*. London: Cassell, 1992.

Herwig, Holger H., and Neil M. Heyman. *Biographical Dictionary of World War I*. Westport, CT: Greenwood Press, 1982.

Hoffman, Robert. *I Remember the Last War*. York, PA: Strength & Health, 1940.

Hook, Alex. *World War I Day by Day*. Rochester, England: Grange Books, 2004.

Hough, Richard. *The Great War at Sea, 1914–1918*. New York: Oxford University Press, 1983.

Howe, Mark Antony De Wolfe. *Memoirs of the Harvard Dead in the War Against Germany*. 5 vols. Cambridge, MA: Harvard University Press, 1920–1925.

✩ Hutchinson. *Dictionary of World War I*. London: Brockhampton Press, 1994.

Jablonski, Edward. *A Pictorial History of the World War I Years*. Garden City, NY, 1979.

Jacks, L. V. *Service Record by an Artilleryman*, 1928.

Jones, Barbara, and Bill Howell. *Popular of the First World War*. New York: McGraw-Hill, 1972.

Keegan, John. *The First World War*. New York: Vintage Books, 1998.

Kennett, Lee. *The First Air War, 1914–1918*. New York: Free Press, 1991.

Kramer, Alan. *Dynamic of Destruction: Culture and Mass Killing in the First World War*. New York: Oxford University Press, 2007.

☆ Laffin, John. *World War I in Post-Cards*. London: Wrens Park, 2001.

Lewis, Cecil. *Sagittarius Rising*. 1936. London: Greenhill Books, 2006.

Longstreet, Stephen. *The Canvas Falcons: The Men and the Planes of World War I*. New York: Barnes & Noble, 1995.

Macdonald, Lyn. *To the Last Man: Spring 1918*. New York: Carroll & Graf, 1998.

Marshall, S. L. A. *World War I*. Boston: Houghton Mifflin, 2001. (Also published as *The American Heritage History of World War I*)

Messenger, Charles, consultant. *World War I in Colour: The Definitive Illustrated History*. London: Ted Smart, 2003.

Meyer, G. J. *A World Undone: The Story of the Great War, 1914–1918*. New York: Delta, 2007.

Mitchell, David. *Monstrous Regiment: The Story of the Women of the First World War*. New York: Macmillan, 1965.

Mosier, John. *The Myth of the Great War: A New Military History of World War I*. New York: Perennial, 2001.

Neillands, Robin. *The Great War Generals on the Western Front, 1914–1918*. London: Magpie Books, 2004.

The 120th Field Artillery Diary, 1880-1919. Milwaukee, WI: Historical Committee, 120th Field Artillery Association, 1928.

O'Shea, Stephen. *Back to the Front: An Accidental Historian Walks the Trenches of World War I*. New York: Avon Books, 1996.

Paris, Michael, ed. *The First World War and Popular Cinema, 1914 to the Present*. New Brunswick, NJ: Rutgers University Press, 2000.

Pope, Stephen, and Elizabeth-Anne Wheal. *The Macmillan Dictionary of the First World War*. New York: Macmillan, 1997.

Prior, Robin, and Trevor Wilson. *The First World War*. London: Cassell, 2001.

Ranlett, Louis Felix. *Let's Go: The Story of A.S. No. 2448602*. Boston: Houghton Mifflin, 1927.

Rendinell, J. E., and George Pattullo. *One Man's War: The Diary of a Leatherneck*. New York: J. H. Sears, 1928.

☆ Ross, Stewart. *Atlas of Conflicts: World War I*. Milwaukee, WI: World Almanac Library, 2004.

Sheffield, Gary, ed. *War on the Western Front*. London: Osprey, 2007.

☆ Snyder, Louis L. *The First Book of World War I*. New York: Franklin Watts, 1958.

☆ Sommerville, Donald. *World War I: History of Warfare*. Austin, TX: Raintree Streck-Vaughn, 1999.

☆ Sparknotes. *World War I, 1914–1919*. New York: Spark Educational Publishing, 2005.

☆ Stewart, Gail B. *People at the Center of World War I*. Farmington Hills, MI: Blackbirch Press, 2004.

Stone, Norman. *World War One*. New York: Basic Books, 2009.

Strachan, Hew, ed. *The Oxford Illustrated History of the First World War*. New York: Oxford University Press, 1998.

☆ Sutton, Felix. *The How and Why Wonder Book of the First World War*. New York: Wonder Books, 1964.

Taylor, A. J. P. *The First World War: An Illustrated History*. New York: Penguin, 1970.

Thomas, Lowell. *Woodfill of the Regulars: A True Story of Adventure from the Arctic to the Argonne*. Garden City, NY: Doubleday, 1929.

Tuchman, Barbara W. *The Guns of August*. 1962. Reprint. New York: Ballantine Books, 1994.

Tucker, Spencer C., ed. *The European Powers in the First World War: An Encyclopedia*. New York: Garland, 1996.

Turner, Pierre, illustrator. *Military Uniforms & Weaponry: The Poster Book of World War I*. New York: Military Press, 1987.

Van Emden, Richard. *Tommy's Ark: Soldiers and Their Animals in the Great War*. London: Bloomsbury, 2010.

Venzon, Anne Cipriano, ed. *The United States in the First World War: An Encyclopedia*. New York: Garland, 1995.

Ward, Candace, ed. *World War One British Poets*. Mineola, NY: Dover, 1997.

Westwell, Ian. *The Complete Illustrated History of World War I*. London: Lorenz Books, 2009.

Westwell, Ian. *World War I: Day by Day*. St. Paul, MN: MBI Publishing, 2004.

Williams, John. *The Other Battleground: The Home Fronts—Britain, France, and Germany, 1914–1918*. Chicago: Henry Regnery, 1972.

Willmott, H. P. *World War I*. New York: DK Publishing, 2008.

Wilson, Bryant, and Lamar Tooze. *With the 364th Infantry in America, France, and Belgium*. New York: Knickerbocker Press, 1919.

Winter, J. M. *The Experience of World War I*. New York: Oxford University Press, 1988.

Wise, Frederick M. *A Marine Tells It to You*. New York: J. H. Sears, 1929.

INDEX